Breathe As If Your
Life Depends On It

By
Rudra Shivananda

Alight Publications
2003

Breathe Like Your Life Depends On It

By Rudra Shivananda

First Edition Published in December, 2003

Alight Publications
PO Box 930
Union City, CA 94587

http://www.i-Alight.com

ISBN 1-931833-04-4

Library of Congress Control Number: 2003195223

Printed in the United States of America

*Dedicated
to the
Naths and Siddhas,
the Masters of Yoga and Life,
whose tireless efforts over millennia,
have preserved and spread
the timeless knowledge
of health,
rejuvenation, and
Self-realization*

Contents

Introduction

Would you be surprised to learn that you have been neglecting your best friend for most of your life? How many of us have paid more than a moment's thought to our breath?

On some level, we are all aware that life ends when breathing stops for more than a few minutes, and yet, we have not paid much attention to the proper maintenance and optimum care of our breath. We take breathing for granted.

My first exposure to the importance of proper breathing was when I read the Science of Breath by *Yogi Ramacharaka* [Arthur Atkinson] back in 1972. It had a profound effect on my understanding of *Hatha Yoga*. Even though it was written almost 100 years ago, it's message that most people have improper breathing habits that are detrimental to their health and spiritual practice is still relevant today.

There has been a marked improvement in the understanding of proper breathing techniques in the West, due to the continuous influx of Eastern teachers, and the culture of physical health being promoted in the United States and other affluent societies for the last thirty years. Unfortunately, there has been a concomitant decrease in the healthy breathing habits of the masses in developing countries, such as India itself, due to the priority given to Western education and application of outdated nineteenth century colonial practices. Today, even in the land of *Yoga* and enlightened sages, school children are taught the unhealthy habit of inhaling, while pulling in the abdomen, without using the diaphragm, restricting the expansion of the lungs and decreasing the amount of air that can reach the body's organs.

Most people still breathe with only about a third of their lung capacity. By learning how to breathe properly to strengthen and extend the respiratory capacity can give a tremendous healing boost to the vital organs which have been habitually starved for oxygen and bathed in carbon dioxide waste. Therefore the first part of the book focuses on developing Breath Awareness, and to learning the practice of the Basic Natural Breath, also called the Full *Yogic* Breath. By regular breathing in a deeper and fuller manner, the quality of one's life will greatly improve. It has been observed that even long-term physiological problems have been healed by the regular practice of the Full *Yogic* Breath

The second part of the book is dedicated to the *Yogic* science and art of breath, called *pranayama*. This is a science because the techniques are based on physiological principles, applicable and with predictable results for all practitioners. However, it is also an art because skillful practice, under the supervision of a qualified mentor is generally required to prevent harmful effects that may occur due to malpractice. In *pranayama*, the laboratory is the practitioner's own body and mind, the state of which can vary over a wide range and complexity, making it impossible to be adequately covered by any textbook. Personal observation, guidance and timely feedback are critical to success.

Most of the major techniques of *pranayama* are introduced in Part Two. These techniques are not new, and have been practiced by countless generations of *yogis* in India. The actual instructions for practice are mostly from oral tradition, but there are useful information given about the techniques in many *Yogic* texts. I've made reference to and quoted some of primary texts, such as the *Tirumandirum* of *Mahasiddha Tirumoolar*, the *Yoga Sutras* of *Mahasiddha Patanajali*, *Hatha Yoga Pradipika* of *Swatmarama* from the *Nath* tradition. The quotes from the *Tirumandirum* are from the Three-volume set translated by Dr. B. Natarajan. The rest of the quotes are from my free-form translations.

A distinctive feature of this presentation of the timeless knowledge of the control and expansion of life-force energy, is that the techniques are given and taught without the forced holding of breath, in apparent contradiction to the classical presentations, translated by scholars. This is because the translated texts were never meant to be used by beginners to practice on their own, but to supplement the oral teachings from a qualified instructor. The instructor would normally give techniques in progressive difficulty, after close observations of the effects on the practitioner, and forced holding of breath is given, only after the student has mastered the basic techniques. Another factor to consider, is that natural breath retention occurs with the sustained correct practice of *Pranayama*, and do not require forcefully and willfully restricting the breath. The benefits of natural breath retention will be explained in greater detail, in the text itself.

For completeness, and for the reference of those who have qualified instruction, the techniques are given with the holding of breath variations, in the appendix.

The usual custom had been to include *pranayama* as a section of most *Hatha* and *Kundalini Yoga* texts, which in most cases did not do full justice to its scope and benefits. A few notable texts, such as Light on *Pranay*ama by BKS Iyengar and recently, The Yoga of Breath by Richard Rosen have given valuable information for new, as well as, seasoned practitioners. One distinctive feature of both of these texts is the emphasis on the use of props, such as supporting blankets, and belts. Another interesting feature is the use of reclining postures for the *pranayama* practices. Another noteworthy text is Science of Breath by *Swami Rama*, which explains in detail the Full Yogic Breath, and basic considerations about breathing properly.

My own tradition is that of the *Nath Yogis* and *Siddhas*, the originators of *Hatha, Kundalini* and *Kriya Yogas*. In line with this tradition, I've given the breathing techniques, without the use of props, and encouraging the practice in sitting postures. The use of props may suit, or be needed by some practitioners, but tend to overshadow the practice itself, unnecessarily, if overly indulged, or relied on. However, if you are already used to the props, then it is best to stick with them, until your instructor tells you otherwise. Personally, I've never practiced breathing techniques, except in various sitting postures, with a fairly relaxed, but straight back, and cannot comment on the usefulness of using reclining, or flat-on-the-back type of postures. It may be worthwhile to remember that *pranayama* is not the control and expansion of breath, but of the life-force energy, and there is an old *yogic* injunction against doing such practices when the spine is against the earth, or not otherwise free.

Breath Awareness can be beneficially extended into a variety of other *yogic* activities, to enhance their effects. Part Three gives examples of the application of Breath Awareness to *yogic* postures, meditation, and healing. A number of techniques for healing of oneself and others, by the application of life-force control are described. The *yogis* have also given us certain useful information in the science of *Swarodaya*, also called *Swara Yoga*. This is a survey and application of the accumulated useful information about the effects on everyday activities that can be caused by the intentional balancing of the vital energy or *prana*, which is carried by the breath.

In the appendix, I've included some information on the three muscular locks, or *bandhas*, which are critical to any *pranayama* practice involving the forced retention of breath. Here also, I've provided the instructions for the *pranayama* variations, involving the forced holding of breath, for the sake of completeness, and for those who have been authorized and guided to such practices.

Throughout this book, I have attempted to provide a thorough and useful overview of the Science and Art of Breath, as preserved and presented by the *Yogic* Masters of India. However, this is by no means an exhaustive treatment of the subject matter, and much is still kept esoteric, to be revealed to the practitioner in the traditional manner. A qualified and experienced mentor is required for the successful incorporation of *pranayama* into a spiritual practice. Notwithstanding the previous statement, I believe that most everyone can benefit from the increase in health and awareness, just from learning the complete *Yogic* breath in Part One, and some of the simple breathing exercises in Part Two, which do not involve the forced breath retention, as well as the practical applications for self-Healing, given in Part Three.

Part 1
Breath Awareness

Rudra Shivananda

Learning how to breathe

We seem to take proper breathing for granted. It is neither taught by parents at home, nor by teachers in schools. In actuality, we all develop bad breathing habits, which can lead to ill-health, but our medical authorities are too focused on prescribing expensive, quick-acting drugs, which work to relieve the symptoms, but do not address the cause of the problems. The best present you can give yourself is learning how to "breathe like your life depends on it!"

We will start by exploring our breath and breathing patterns. The key to optimizing one's influx of oxygen and life-force is through abdominal breathing. You will be able to look out for the incorrect methods of exhalation and inhalation, while learning the correct method. This abdominal breathing also reduces stress and increases calmness and peace of mind, by lowering the heart rate.

In teaching and advising many students on breathing techniques over the years, there is a consistent reluctance among both men and women to expand their abdomen during inhalation. It seems to be driven by our anxieties over having an extended abdomen. Our popular culture applauds and hungers after a flat, 'wash-board' abdomen. You will be glad to know that the proper healthy breathing techniques do not contribute to 'beer-belly'. Rather, the Full *Yogic* Breath, which will be introduced later in the chapter, helps to tone your abdominal muscles.

It is amazing and gratifying to observe the improvements in the quality of life among those who spend just fifteen minutes a day on improving their breath awareness.

Find a comfortable, preferably carpeted floor, and put a sheet on it. Lie down on the floor on your back, relax, and observe the motion of your breath. Let your hands rest at your sides, palms facing up, and with legs separated enough to relax your lower back. Begin by observing your natural breathing pattern. Be mindful of the air as it enters your nostrils.

As you inhale, watch where it expands, and as you exhale, watch where it releases. Be aware of the rate and pace of your breath, and the difference between inhalation and exhalation. Your breathing pattern may vary at different times of the day. Many factors contribute to your breathing pattern, as you will find out, once you relax and become more aware. Some of the major factors which affect breathing, include emotion, physical activity and mental state.

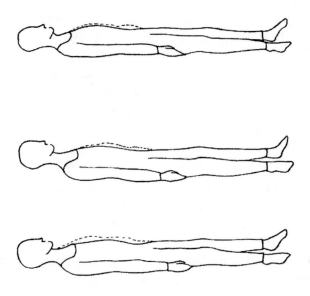

Figure 1. Abdominal Breathing: Lying down

Feel the interior spaces as your breath enters your head and begins its interior journey down through your trachea into your lungs. Become aware of where you feel the natural motions of your breathing. Does it feel labored or effortless? Do you notice one particular area receiving the breath more than some other regions? You may also be able to distinguish a temperature difference between the inhalation and the exhalation as it moves through your nostrils.

Now focus on your abdominal area, allowing a gentle expansion there as you inhale. Then let it contract and sink inward as you exhale. It is useful to place your hands on your lower abdomen and gently compress your abdominal muscles as you exhale.

When pressure is applied to the middle abdomen during exhalation, a parasympathetic reflex is activated, which will decrease the heart rate and lower blood pressure. The pressure on the abdomen is picked up by a sensor in the aorta which in turn signals the hypothalamus in the mid-brain. The hypothalamus is responsible for regulating heart rate and blood pressure. You will find that abdominal breathing is an effective method to relax.

Continue this abdominal breathing for at least five minutes, to fully feel the calming effect, and benefit from stress relief.

Next, during inhalation, after the expansion of the abdomen, focus on the chest area, and feel the movement of the ribs, outward and upward. Feel the chest expand, with the inhalation, and compress, with the exhalation. Co-ordinate the abdominal breathing with the chest breathing, in a smooth movement, without jerks or strain.

Perform this breathing pattern for at least five minutes, before getting up, off the ground.

After this experience of abdominal breathing lying down, you are ready to observe the same movement in a sitting position. Sit at the edge of a chair, and focus on the abdominal area, expanding it as you inhale, and compressing it as you exhale.

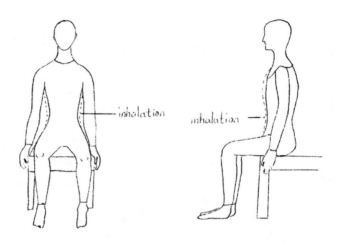

Figure 2. Abdominal Breathing: sitting position

The next stage in breath awareness is to observe and visualize the movement of the diaphragm that separates the chest from the abdomen, and applying the correct abdominal control.

Inhale: Your diaphragm goes down as air rushes into your lungs. The action of the diaphragm widens your rib cage and also pushes your intestines downward and forward.

Figure 3A shows the incorrect way, because it lets the abdomen move outwards like a balloon. There is no pressure placed on the internal organs, and there may be congestion due to too much blood accumulating in the viscera.

Figure 3B shows the correct abdominal breath. After the diaphragm has reached its lowest position, the abdominal muscles provide a counter pressure. There is no abnormal swelling or deformation of the abdomen.

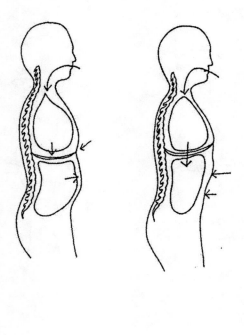

3A   *3B*

Figure 3. Incorrect [3A] and Correct [3B] Inhalation

Exhale: Your diaphragm returns to its original position, and air is expelled from your lungs. Your abdomen withdraws and moves up when you breathe out.

Without abdominal control, the organs are not compressed, since the abdominal muscles are passively following the exhalation. This is shown in figure 4A. The correct way is to contract the abdominal muscles at the end of exhalation, consciously pushing the internal organs upwards, expelling the maximum residual air, as shown in figure 4B.

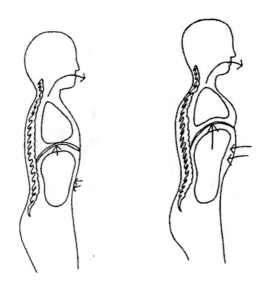

4A   **4B**
Figure 4. Incorrect [4A] and Correct [4B] Exhalation

Rudra Shivananda

Unfortunately, many people do not breathe in the manner that has been described. Instead they swell the belly during exhalation and contract the abdomen during inhalation. This reverse breathing is due to the exaggerated use of the chest, neck, and shoulders. This breathing pattern often causes chronic tension in the neck and shoulders and irregular biological rhythms – menstrual flow, frequent urination, and insomnia.

When people regain their natural pattern of abdominal breathing, most of the symptoms of chronic stress fade away. This healing effect of stress relief, is not only due to the decrease in neck and shoulder strain, and the increase in oxygen to the lungs, but also to the increase in *prana* or life-force, which is carried by the breath. Part Two will cover the details about the control and extension of this *prana*.

However, changing deficient breathing patterns require persistent practice, and not only a superficial understanding of the breathing mechanism. Once you've experienced the best way to breathe, putting it into practice will be the goal of the rest of this chapter.

In order to understand the mechanism of breathing, it will be useful to look at the organs of respiration, as well as the chemical control of the process. Although we can breathe without knowing anything about the mechanics, for fuller control and rectification of any bad habits, such knowledge is helpful.

The Physical organs of the respiratory system

The nose and pharynx

The nose is divided into two nostrils by a nasal septum. The nostrils are lined with mucous membranes that serve to moisten the air and filter out any heavy particles that might become trapped and may be harmful to the internal organs. The nostrils are also lined with a single layer of cells, containing small hair like projections called cilia that act to change the direction of the airflow and heighten its speed. The breath passes through a series of pathways in the nose that act like turbines to increase the speed and direct the flow of the breath toward the deeper lobes of the lungs. They also permit a warming of the air immediately before entering the pharynx on the way to the trachea.

Most *Yogic* breathing exercise require the use of the nose, rather than mouth, because with mouth breathing, the mucous membranes in the throat dry out, increasing the risk of irritation and infection. Become aware of the difference between mouth and nostril breathing. Which is easier and more natural?

The pharynx is a muscular tube that lies behind the nose and mouth, opening into the larynx in front, and the esophagus [the food channel] in the back. The muscles of the pharynx are used chiefly for swallowing.

Larynx

This is composed of pieces of cartilage , and in particular on top is a small piece called epiglottis which closes the passage during swallowing allowing the food to pass into the food canal rather than the trachea or wind-pipe.

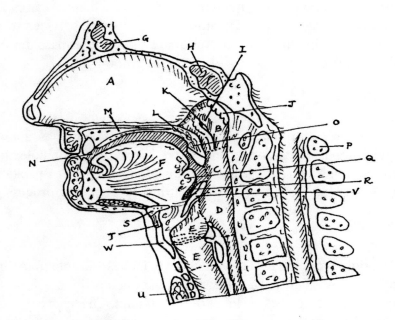

A Nasal Septum	G Frontal Sinus	N Oral Cavity	U Throid Gland
B Nasophrynx	H Sphenoidal sinus	O Uvula	V Epiglottis
C Orophrynx	I Tubal tonsil	P Spine	W Thyroid
D Laryngophrynx	J Phryngeal tonsil	Q Lingual tonsil	Cartilage
E Larynx	K Opening of auditory	R Vallecula	
F Tongue	L Soft palate	S Hyoid Bone	
	M Hard palate	T Thyrohyoid Mrmbtsnr	

Figure 5. Nasal Cavity and Trachea

Vocal Chords

There are two pairs of mucous membrane folds in the larynx. The lower or inferior folds are the true vocal folds or cords. The upper or superior folds are the false vocal cords. Only the true cords create sound, vibrating like violin strings in the air stream. The glottis consists of the true cords and the opening between them. By constricting the glottis, a variable amount of air pass through the voice box.

Trachea

This is a pipe formed by an incomplete ring of cartilages, about 4 inches long, which divides into the right and left bronchi, leading to the lungs. The trachea has to maintain a degree of plasticity under varying thoracic pressures during the breathing process.

Bronchi

The right bronchus divides into three branches and enter into three lobes of the right lung, while the left bronchus divides into two branches to enter the two lobes of the left lung. The most important part of the bronchus is the thin circular layer of smooth muscle which runs all around it. When this muscle contracts, the bronchial passage is restricted, and when it relaxes, the passage is expanded.

The lungs and the alveoli or air sacs

The two lungs fill the chest cavity, separated in the middle by the heart and its blood vessels. They are pear shaped, with smaller upper lobes and larger lower lobes. The upper lobes can extend. The lower lungs are wider than the upper lungs when viewed from the front, and they fill the entire width of the middle rib cage. The bottoms of the lungs are concave, conforming to the shape of the diaphragm's dome.

It is at the single layer of cells in the alveoli that the blood comes into closest contact with the air. Oxygen diffuses from the inhaled air in the air sac into the slowly moving blood circulating around the air sacs.

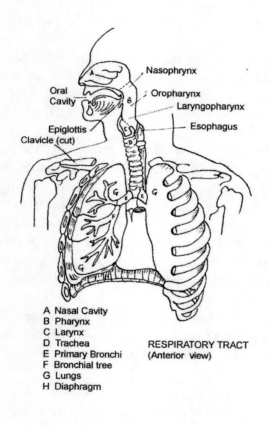

Oral Cavity

Nasophrynx

Oropharynx

Laryngopharynx

Esophagus

Epiglottis
Clavicle (cut)

A Nasal Cavity
B Pharynx
C Larynx
D Trachea
E Primary Bronchi
F Bronchial tree
G Lungs
H Diaphragm

RESPIRATORY TRACT
(Anterior view)

Figure 6. Respiratory Tract: Anterior View

The diaphragm and intercostals muscles

The diaphragm is the domed-shaped sheet of muscle lining the floor of the chest cavity. Contraction of the diaphragm enlarges the chest cavity in the downward direction.

The Intercostal muscles are two oblique strips of muscle in-between the ribs. Contraction of these muscles causes the elevation of the rib-cage and the expansion of the chest outward.

The muscles of the neck attached to the clavicles also play a part in the breathing process. The contraction of these muscles pull up the sternum and clavicle to expand the chest in the upward direction.

Figure 7 shows that the diaphragm divides the heart and lungs from the digestive organs below it. It is the major muscle of respiration. This large flat muscle is shaped somewhat like a full parachute or a dome. The diaphragm's motion is similar to that of a piston, just as the lungs are similar to a combustion chamber. During inhalation, the diaphragm contracts and moves downward, pulling air inward. During shallow breathing, air does not enter the lungs' larger lower regions, while with a full inhalation, air reaches into the lower lungs, where there is more space to receive the full capacity of respiration. During exhalation, the diaphragm relaxes upward and back to its dome shape, allowing for the release of carbon dioxide and other metabolic waste gases.

With *Yogic* breathing, the three sets of muscles, the diaphragm, intercostals and neck muscles, will be strengthened to enable more air to move in and out during a normal respiratory cycle. Thus, the effects of *pranayama* training will last throughout the day. The quantity of circulating air (called the tidal volume) is increased and the number of breaths per minute is decreased, leading to the development of a more efficient respiratory system.

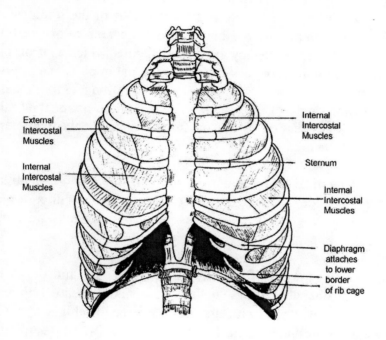

External
Intercostal
Muscles

Internal
Intercostal
Muscles

Internal
Intercostal
Muscles

Sternum

Internal
Intercostal
Muscles

Diaphragm
attaches
to lower
border
of rib cage

Figure 7. Diaphragm and Intercostal muscles

Control of Breathing

Respiration is regulated and controlled by the nervous system, as well as by the chemical balance in the blood.

The respiratory center is a group of nerve cells in the medulla oblongata, situated in the lower part of the brain stem. This center maintains the basic automatic respiratory reflex. However, it is influenced by the Hypothalamus, which controls the whole autonomic nervous system. Emotional impulses can cause the Hypothalamus to signal to the medulla oblongata to increase the rate and depth of the breath. The frontal cortex of the brain also has a connection to the medullar center for the voluntary control of the breath.

Chemical changes in the blood will signal to the medullar center to change the breathing rate. Too much carbon dioxide and insufficient oxygen will stimulate an increase in the rate and depth of breathing.

As you know from experience, the rate and depth of respiration changes increase with exercise and decrease with rest. The normal rate varies with age, and gender, with a higher rate for younger people and women. It varies from the 10-20 times/minute for an adult to the 40 times per minute of a new-born baby.

The Mechanisms of Breathing

The ancient masters of breath have classified four different methods of breathing:

- Abdominal or diaphragmatic or low breathing
- Intercostal or middle breathing
- Clavicular or upper breathing
- Complete *Yogic* breathing

Abdominal Breathing consists of the movement of the diaphragm and of the outer wall of the abdomen. As you inhale the diaphragm muscle is flattened from a dome shape to a disc shape, as it moves downwards. This compresses the abdominal organs and eventually pushes the front wall, the navel and the abdomen outwards. This movement acts as a massage to the upper abdominal organs, such as liver, stomach, transverse large intestine, and pancreas. With practice, it will also massage the mid-abdominal organs, particularly, the ascending and descending large intestine and the centrally located small intestines. The abdominal muscles must relax for this to occur, causing a slight swelling of the belly. A counter pressure from the abdomen is applied, once the diaphragm has reached its maximum position.

As you exhale, the abdominal muscles contract more and the diaphragm moves upwards, reducing the volume in the chest cavity, and relaxing back into a dome shape, mildly compressing the lungs and heart. The contractions during abdominal breathing tone the centrally located rectus abdominis muscle, strengthening it to move more air in and out, and increasing the quantity of air circulating within the body (called the tidal volume) and reducing the number of breaths per minute. Abdominal breathing is physiologically the most efficient because it draws in the greatest amount of air for the least amount of muscular effort.

In Intercostal Breathing, the movement of the ribs becomes the focus. The rib movements are caused by two sets of muscles between the ribs: the internal and external intercostals. These muscles depress and narrow the rib cage during exhalation. During inhalation, the intercostals reverse the process to expand the rib cage's diameter, increasing the internal cavity space to allow the lungs to expand, resulting in air being drawn down into them from the front side..

In Clavicular Breathing, inhalation and deflation of the lungs is achieved by raising the upper ribs, shoulders and collarbones (clavicles). Very little air is inhaled and exhaled, since this movement cannot change the volume of the chest cavity very much, requiring maximum effort to obtain minimum benefit.

This upper breathing is common in our society, owing to the modern lifestyles we have adopted in the cities where we are subjected to stressful conditions – noise, pollution, badly ventilated rooms and offices, as well as second-hand smoke. The competitive work arena contributes further to the state of anxiety, immobilizing the diaphragm in an attempt to deal with the deep-seated fears of aggression and other deep emotional feelings, causing harmful shallow breathing.

Complete natural or *Yogic* Breathing combines all the above three methods of breathing into one complete harmonious movement. The entire respiratory system is brought into full use, exercising all the respiratory muscles including the internal and external intercostals and abdominal muscles, as well as the rib cage, the lungs and their air sacs, and the diaphragm. Our goal should be to develop this type of complete breathing which can give the maximum benefit for the body.

Yogic Energization

There is a set of exercises which are very beneficial for energizing the body, as well as opening up the lungs. These are done in the early morning, before the breathing exercises.

These simple exercises are based on the fact that tensing a muscle, restricts energy flow to it, while relaxing the same muscle, enables energy to flow unimpeded to it. An additional advantage for beginners, is that instead of tensing and relaxing individual muscles, the tension is initiated by pressing a pair of muscles together, isometrically.

The *yogis* of the Himalayas have pioneered the use of such "isometric" techniques, millennia before the West discovered them. They are generally easier to learn and perform than the traditional yogic postures. This set also stretches and loosens up the spine, for easing the upward flow of energy.

The key to performing these exercises, is to bring your awareness, into every movement, and to seamlessly integrate your breath with the movements, according to the instructions.

Energization 1

Stand straight with hands by your side. Eyes are softly focused ahead. Become aware of the body. Become aware of the air passing through your nostrils. Feel your feet sink into the floor.

As you inhale, bring your arms to the sides. Palms are facing down. Exhale slowly, and feel the connection of the palm with the earth.

Inhale, sweeping your arms overhead, with the palms, pressing against each other. Hold you breath for a few seconds, as you stretch up, balancing on your toes. Elongate the spine. Focus on the tension in your palms, and tighten every muscle of the body.

Exhale slowly, and lower your arms, relaxing your muscles. Feel the energy rushing into your arms and shoulders, and the opening of the chest and lungs.

Repeat two more times.

Energization 2

Stand straight with hands by your side. Eyes are softly focused ahead. Become aware of the body. Become aware of the air passing through your nostrils. Feel your feet sink into the floor.

As you inhale, bring your arms to the sides. Palms are facing down. Exhale slowly, and feel the connection of the palm with the earth.

Inhale, sweeping your arms overhead, with the **back of the palms**, pressing against each other. Hold you breath for a few seconds, as you stretch up, balancing on your toes. Elongate the spine. Focus on the tension in your palms, and tighten every muscle of the body.

Exhale slowly, and lower your arms, relaxing your muscles. Feel the energy rushing into the back of the arms and the area around the shoulder-blades.

Repeat two more times.

Energization 3

Stand with feet shoulder-width apart. Arms are by the side. Eyes are focused on the tip of the nose. Palms are facing outward. Become aware of the breath, and the palms.

Inhale, stretching arms up, and overhead. Lock the thumbs together, with the left thumb on top of the right, pulling one thumb against the other, to create tension. Balance on the tips of your toes.

Exhale, and bend slowly to the left side, keeping the elbows in line with the ears. Hold the breath out for a few seconds, as you feel the tension along the right side of the body, from the right toes, to the right thumb.

Inhale and return to the upright position, keeping arms overhead, and thumbs interlocked. Repeat the left-bend two more times, and then relax arms to the sides. Become aware of the movement of the energy, during the relaxation.

Inhale, stretching arms overhead. Lock the thumbs, with the right thumb on top of the left, pulling one thumb against the other, to create tension.

Exhale, and bend slowly to the right side, keeping the elbows in line with the ears. Hold the breath out for a few seconds, as you feel the tension along the left side of the body, from the left toes, to the left thumb.

Inhale and return to the upright position, Repeat the right-bend two more times, and then relax arms to the sides. Become aware of the movement of the energy, during the relaxation.

Energization 4

Stand straight with hands by your side. Eyes are softly focused ahead. Become aware of the body. Become aware of the air passing through your nostrils. Feel your feet sink into the floor.

Focus your eyes just above the ridge of the nose, between the eyebrows. Clasp your thumbs behind your back, with the left thumb on top of the right.

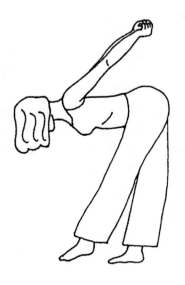

Inhale, and step forward with the left foot. Exhale, and bend forward. lifting your arms as high as possible. Slowly, left the chin up, to feel the tension in the throat, and lower abdomen. Hold this position, with the breath out, for a few moments. Return to the upright position, as you inhale.

Relax, but keep the thumbs together. Repeat the movement two more times, and then return to the beginning stance. Relax completely, feeling the movemnt of energy.

Clasp your thumbs behind your back, this time, with the right one on top.

Step out with the right leg, on the inhalation. Bend forward with the exhalation, and continue as before, for three repetitions.

Completely relax, and become aware of the flow of energy.

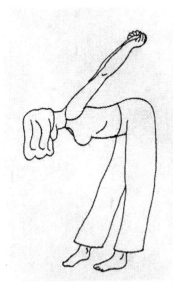

Energization 5

Stand straight with hands by your side, and feet together. Eyes are softly focused ahead. Become aware of the body. Become aware of the air passing through your nostrils. Feel your feet sink into the floor. As you start your inhalation, bring your palms together at the heart level, pressing them together. Continue to raise the arms overhead.

Lean back slowly, while holding the breath, dropping the head back. Arch the back carefully, maintaining tension in the arms. Focus on the sacrum, as you tense the hold body, for a few moments.

Exhale slowly, releasing all tension, passing through the upright position, and bending forward. The arms are parallel to the ground. Feel the stretch in the arms and spine, accompanied by the movement of energy.

Return to the starting position and repeat two more times. Then release your arms to your sides, and completely relax.

Energization 6

Stand straight with hands by your side, and feet together. Eyes are softly focused ahead. Become aware of the body. Become aware of the air passing through your nostrils. Feel your feet sink into the floor. Focus your awareness at the navel.

Inhale and press the arms against the sides of the body.

As you begin exhalation, relax the tension, and swing the right arm up to eye-level, bending the elbow. At the same time, swing the left arm to the left back-side, bending the left elbow. Swing from the waist, to the left, as far as comfortable. Hold the breath out in this position, for a few moments only. Then return to the first position, with the inhalation. Repeat two more times.

Begin exhalation, and swing the left arm up to eye-level, bending the elbow. Simulataneously, swing the right arm to the lower back. Swing to the right, from the waist. Hold the breath out, in this position, for a few seconds. Then inhale back to the starting position. Repeat two more times. Then relax completely, feeling the energy.

Breathing exercise No. 1: Vase Breathing

This is a preliminary breathing exercise that is helpful for you to start getting in touch with the various muscles and modes of breathing. However, keep in mind that this breathing exercise is not a replacement for the more forceful and beneficial Complete *Yogic* Breath that will be introduced in the next section. In fact, the sequence of the breathing movement is opposite between the two, but both uses the same sets of muscles. Vase breathing is gentle and peaceful.

In Vase Breathing, the basic pattern is as follows:

Inhale through the nose: expand your chest first and then let your breath descend like filling a vase to your lower abdomen.
Exhale through the nose: allow your abdomen to go in, pulling in and up on your musculature, then let the air return upward.

The goal of this exercise is an evenness of motion in all three sections of the breath – chest, rib cage, and abdomen. It requires you to be relatively still in order to feel the effect. Thus, it is best learned in a seated position. This vase breathing moves all of the respiratory muscles to full capacity in a passive manner, preventing stress or aggravation to any pre-existing health conditions, while at the same time, healing the underlying physical and emotional tensions.

Sit in a comfortable posture, either cross-legged or on the floor or at the edge of a chair, with the spine straight. All breathing is done through the nose.

During inhalations, let your chest expand first, then let the expansion progress to the lower ribs, and finally into the abdomen. Inhalation is essentially a descending vertical motion. With this descent, the lower rib cage widens and the upper abdominal organs are displaced downward and forward. As in abdominal breathing, there is a mild expansion of the abdomen at the end of the inhalation.

The exhalation is the reverse sequence of the inhalation. The motion is an ascending vertical flow of breath. Begin by first letting the lower abdominal muscles contract to propel the exhaled air from the bottom of the lungs. During the mid range of exhalation, the lower rib cage narrows to promote the ascent of the diaphragm, back to its dome shape.

Maintain a consistent rhythm, feeling fuller and deeper, feeling more internal than external motion. The breathing cycle should be slowed to 8 to 10 breaths per minute, rather than the average 12 to 15 per minute. Your breathing should be so gentle that it is silent to others. Your lower jaw should be relaxed, with your teeth slightly separated, allowing your face to be relaxed and calm.

Once you have experienced and internalized this form of breathing, you will be able to move on to the subtler components of the breath, as well as to appreciate and practice the next exercise. This vase breathing is an invigorating exercise that brings your body to rest, while simultaneously promoting mental clarity.

Practice Vase Breathing twice a day for ten minutes. Do this for a week, before proceeding to the Complete Yogic Breath, so that you can appreciate the differences.

Breathing Exercise No. 2: Complete Yogic Breath

Sit in a comfortable posture, either cross-legged on the floor or at the edge of a chair, with the spine straight. All breathing should be performed through the nostrils and not through the mouth, in a warm and well-ventilated room.

Abdominal and diaphragmatic breathing

Place the palms of your hands lightly on your abdomen. This is to make you aware of the movement in your abdomen as the air is breathed in and out of the lowest lobes of your lungs. Breathe out slowly and completely, becoming aware of the movement of your diaphragm that is responsible for your abdominal breathing. As you exhale, feel your abdomen contract and your navel moving back towards the spine. At the end of exhalation the diaphragm will be totally relaxed and will be doming or parachuting upwards into the chest cavity.

Now, inhale, keeping your chest and shoulders still. Expand the abdomen and feel the navel moving outwards and upwards. The breathing should be deep and slow. At the end of the inhalation your diaphragm will be bowing in the direction of the abdomen and your navel will be as high as it can move.

Exhale again, slowly and completely, contracting the abdomen. Then without any holding of breath, inhale and then repeat the whole process twice more, for a total of three abdominal breaths.

Now move your hands around to your back, so that your palms are resting on your lower back, with the fingers pointing towards the spine. Perform three more abdominal breaths, concentrating your mind on the movement of the lungs, as sensed by your lightly resting hands.

Rudra Shivananda

Intercostal and lower rib breathing

We will now exercise the intercostals muscles. Throughout this practice, keep the abdomen still by slightly contracting the abdominal muscles.

Place your hand on either side of the middle rib cage, so that the fingers of each palm are pointing towards each other. This will help you feel the expansion and contraction of the ribs. Remember that the intercostals are the muscles between the ribs.

Inhale slowly by expanding the rib cage outwards and upwards. You will find it impossible to breathe deeply because of the limitation on the maximum expansion of the chest.

Slowly exhale by contracting the chest downwards and inwards. Keep the abdomen slightly contracted, but without strain.

Breathe in slowly, repeating the whole process two more times.

Now, place your hands behind the mid-area of your back, opposite to where you had your hands placed on your front.

Concentrate and breathe into the middle back area using the rib muscles for another three rounds.

Clavicular or upper breathing

In this exercise, try your best not to move the abdomen or the intercostals, keeping them slightly contracted, but immobile.

Place both palms on your upper chest, so that you can determine whether your chest is moving or not, while trying not to contract the muscles of your abdomen.

[38]

Inhale by drawing your collarbones and shoulders upwards towards your chin, similar to a shrugging movement. If you have difficulty with this movement, try to inhale and exhale with a sniffing action, which automatically induces upper breathing.

Exhale by letting your shoulders and collarbones move downwards away from your chin.

Do this clavicular breathing two more times.

Now, raise your arms over your shoulders, and breathe deeply and slowly into the upper lobes of the lungs, feeling the movement and breath under the armpits.

Perform this three times with concentration and awareness, but without strain.

Complete Yogic Breath

This is a combination of the three previous exercises, taking the maximum volume of air into the lungs and expelling the maximum amount of carbon dioxide.

Breathe out deeply, contracting the abdomen to squeeze all the air from the lungs.

Now, inhale slowly, keeping the lowest part of the abdomen slightly contracted, while expanding the part above the navel. The slight contraction of the lowest abdomen is to help you get over the fear of getting a pot-belly due to the abdominal organs moving down.

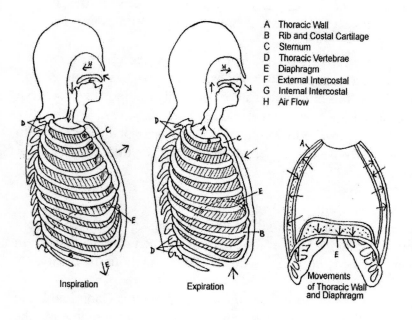

A   Thoracic Wall
B   Rib and Costal Cartilage
C   Sternum
D   Thoracic Vertebrae
E   Diaphragm
F   External Intercostal
G   Internal Intercostal
H   Air Flow

Inspiration   Expiration   Movements
of Thoracic Wall
and Diaphragm

Figure 8. Complete Yogic Breath Movement

At the end of the upper abdomen expansion, start to expand your chest and rib cage outwards and upwards. Continue drawing the breath upwards into the higher lobes of your lungs by raising your collarbones and shoulders towards your chin. Your lungs should now be completely filled with air.

Then, without holding your breath or interrupting the continuous nature of the breathing pattern, begin to exhale, first relaxing your collarbones and shoulders. Then allow your chest to move first downwards and then inwards. Finally, contract the abdomen. Do not strain but try to empty your lungs as much as possible, squeezing all the air out by drawing the abdominal wall closer to the spine.

This completes one round of *Yogic* breathing. Continue for another six rounds. If you need to rest between the rounds, you may take a few "normal" breaths, before continuing.

Practice this breathing exercise for ten minutes, twice a day for the next two weeks, and observe the changes in your energy level. Make this breathing pattern your daily routine, if you observe increase in your energy level and reduction in stress. Your quality of life will be markedly improved when you adopt the *Yogic* Breath as your daily wake-up recipe, rather than relying on that cup of coffee!

The Complete *Yogic* Breath should be one continuous movement, each phase of breathing merging into the next, without there being any physical jerks, strain or even obvious transition point. The body should remain relaxed throughout the practice.

After some practice you will find that this Complete *Yogic* Breath will become second nature to you. Begin to develop the habit of consciously breathing whenever you can throughout the day. If you feel tired, depressed, angry or anxious, then center yourself, sit down, and practice *yogic* breathing. Breathe deeply and slowly with your concentration on the breath. Feel that you are inhaling not just air, but courage, strength, and peace. As you exhale, breathe away any negative qualities that your mind may be holding on to. Then your mind will become calm and revitalized

Besides the emotional and mental benefits, the Complete *Yogic* Breath develops good healthy lung tissues that resist germs, making you much less susceptible to disease. The blood receives plenty of oxygen and every organ of the body is nourished by it. Digestion and assimilation are improved, and bodily energy and vigor are increased.

The Physical health benefits of Breath Training and Therapy

When you watch an infant sleeping, it is easy to determine that it is breathing primarily by using the diaphragm because you can see the abdomen rise and fall, with each breath. It would stand to reason that teaching chronically ill adults to practice diaphragmatic breathing, rather than habitual chest pattern breathing, could restore their health, given what we have discussed so far about the oxygenation benefits of the Complete *Yogic* Breath.

Indeed, researches in China, India and Russia have shown that over 90% of the patients with peptic ulcers can be successfully treated with breathing exercises. Russian research [Kreme Sanatorium] has also have shown successful treatment of tuberculosis patients, while Indian research supports the treatment of patients with hypertension.

Much more research, especially in the United States would be needed to uncover all the potential health benefits of Breath Training and Therapy.

However, we do not need to wait for the results from modern researchers to confirm the insights of thousands of years of yogic science, or what can be confirmed by your own efforts for a few weeks!

Breath and Emotional Release

Have you noticed that when you are depressed, your posture slumps and your breathing becomes constricted? When we are happy, we tend to stand taller and breathe more fully. It appears that our breathing varies with our moods. As you become more aware of your breathing, you will become more aware of your emotional states, and the quality of your thoughts.

Awareness of the emotions does not by itself provide a relief. Noticing your depression or anger does not make them go away. The Complete *Yogic* Breath can be used to help release the negative emotions, and strengthen the positive ones

The process is to first uncover the underlying emotion. Then decide on an antidote – the opposing or healing emotion. Now, with every exhalation, consciously release and expel the negative emotion, while with every inhalation, breath in the positive emotion. The *Yogic* breathing will first bring calm and then a sense of control and eventually joy. Repeat an affirmation which suggests the emotion, such as, "I feel more and more joy [or love etc.]"

However, this breathing release of emotions can only be a short-term healing, unless the underlying behavior that is supporting the negative emotions are modified. This takes deeper awareness, insight, and a high degree of self-discipline, as taught in the practice of meditation.

Caution against the holding of breath

There is a lot of misunderstanding about the practice of breath retention or holding of breath, due to the popularization of advanced *Yogic* texts, which appear to promote this practice indiscriminately. In general, holding of breath can put a stress on your heart and circulatory system, elevating the blood pressure several times above normal, which can result in ruptured blood vessels or a stroke.

What may not be clear from books is that beginners in *Yoga* are not taught the holding of breath, until they have had years of practice in strengthening the body, circulatory system and nervous systems, and only after authorization and personal supervision from their teachers. When holding of breath is taught, it should always be accompanied by the practice of the muscular locks or *bandhas*. More on this subject is given in the Appendix of this book.

It is my personal experience and observation, that most breathing techniques do not require the active and forced breath retention, but will over time, increase the natural pause between the inhaled breath and the exhaled breath. This natural pause does not put a strain on the heart.

Part 2
The Yogic
Science and Art
of Breath :
Pranayama

In the first part, we have learnt how to enhance our lives through simply being aware of our breath. By unlearning any bad habits and cultivating the optimum way to breathe – the Full *Yogic* Breath, you have felt the difference in energy level and health.

We will now delve deeper into the study of life-force or *prana*. The *yogic* sages of India, as part of their comprehensive insight into the psycho-energetic properties of the human body-mind-soul complex, have left us a rich legacy of knowledge about the control and expansion of this life-force. Many modern practitioners have benefited greatly from even a casual understanding of this treasury of knowledge.

The *Naths* and *Hatha Yoga*

The *Naths* are the perennial upholders of the *Sanatana Dharma*, or *Yogic* Evolutionary Path. From time immemorial, they have instructed humanity in the ways of self-realization. They are the Lords of Yoga, and in more recent times, have been called the *Siddhas*, or "perfected beings".

From the period of around 600 CE to 900 CE, the immortal, *Gorakshanath*, whose deeds blur the lines between myth, legend and history, initiated the path of *Hatha Yoga*, giving greater prominence to the practice of developing life-force energy. He took this step, to give aid to humanity, in the midst of a dark age, which made it difficult for spiritual aspirants to practice the higher steps of meditation directly. The science and art of breath expansion and control was given the prominent role in healing and self-realization.

In the West, *Hatha Yoga*, has been erroneously equated with the physical postures, which are practiced for a healthy and stable body. *Hatha* is the union of the Sun and the Moon, or the hot and cool energy channels in the astral body, and is the essence of what later came to be called *Kundalini Yoga*. As this is an esoteric teaching, we will explain and explore this subject, in a later section, after we've covered some of the foundation concepts, such as the *nadis* [energy channels], *chakras* [energy centers], *prana* [life-force energy], and *Kundalini* [potential awakening energy].

Under the direction of *Shiva-Goraksha-Babaji* [another name for *Gorakshanath*], the *yogis* began to teach and practice *Hatha Yoga*, throughout the medieval times. One of them, another immortal, *Sundarnath*, went to Southern India, and as *Tirumoolar*, became a pillar of light in the South. Our main sources for the practice of *pranayama* date from the 14th century and onwards, when there was great disruption and turmoil in India, due to Muslim invaders, and the teachings had to be written down for fear of being lost.

It is important to keep in mind that *Hatha Yoga* is practiced for moving into the higher states of meditation, and not for its own sake, or for the sake of attaining the *siddhis* or psychic powers. This has firmly been stated in the second verse of the well-known text, called *Hatha Yoga Pradipika*, "The knowledge of *Ha* and *Tha* is given solely for the sake of attaining to *Raja Yoga*".

The Texts of Pranayama

There are no specific texts dealing only on *pranayama*. The techniques are given in the *Hatha Yoga* texts.

Goraksha-Paddhati:
An authoritative text of *Hatha Yoga*, consisting of 202 stanzas. It is also the fountainhead for the practice of *Kundalini Yoga*, being one of the earliest texts giving techniques for arousing *Kundalini* energy. A selection of 100 verses from the *Goraksha-Paddhati* is called **Goraksha-Shataka**.

Figure 9. Immortal Gorakshanath

Tirumandirum:
Over 3000 verses covering all aspects of the *yogic* path, composed by *Sundarnath*, a disciple of *Gorakshanath*, who, as the story goes, while visiting South India, took the body of a dead cow-herd and stayed to instruct the Tamil people, as the *Siddhar Tirumoolar*.

Figure 10. Immortal Siddhar Tirumoolar

Hatha-Yoga Pradipika:
The most popular manual on *Hatha Yoga*, composed in the 14th century, by *Yogi Swatmarama*, and dedicated to *Gorakshanath* and the *Nath* tradition. This was written as a notebook for practitioners and consists of basic descriptions of most of the fundamental techniques, including the most often practiced *pranayamas*.

Gheranda-Samhita:
A late 17th century work, which borrows heavily from the *Pradipika*. The extensive purification techniques given in this text are of interest to yogic practitioners of *pranayama*, because, for the free flow of *prana* or life-force, the body centers and channels should be cleansed and purified.

Yoga Vashishta:
A large work of 30,000 verses, written in poetic from. Although primarily dealing with the exposition of the path of knowledge, or Jnana Yoga, there is also very useful information on the practice of pranayama, particularly from the less forceful and gentler perspective.

Yoga-Sutras of Patanjali:
The most widely known yogic text, attributed to the *yogic* sage *Patanjali*, from the 2nd century BCE. This timeless spiritual masterpiece does not give specific techniques of *pranayama*, but outlines an eight-fold practice, or *Ashtanga*, with *pranayama* being the 4th limb, leading to self-realization.

What is Pranayama?

Pranayama is the Sanskrit term for the *yogic* science and art of breathing. It is formed from two root words *prana* and *ayama*. *Prana* means a "subtle life-force" which gives energy to the mind and body, and *ayama* signifies the voluntary effort to control, direct and expand this *prana*.

Pranayama is both a physical process of regulating the breath voluntarily as well as the subtle expansion of the *prana*. It is the union of the individual *prana* with the Universal *Prana*, and forms an integral part of *Yoga*, the science of self-realization.

In contrast to Part 1, where very few Sanskrit terms were introduced, the exposition of this science, requires an exposure to the yogic terms, which are necessary to understand the deeper levels of the subject matter.

The first purpose of *pranayama* is to improve the health and prolong the life of the body, in order that the aspiring *yogi* can have a better life and longer time to perfect his practice and reach his goal.

The second purpose is to purify the subtle energy channels, the *nadis*, in the subtle energy body called the *pranamayakosa*, in order to allow *prana* to flow into the central *nadi*, called *sushumna*.

The third purpose is as a lead-in for meditation or *dhyana*, as mental fluctuations are eliminated with the balancing of *prana*.

The basic parts or movements of *pranayama* are *puraka* (inhalation), *rechaka* (exhalation) and *kumbhaka* (retention of the breath).

Rudra Shivananda

Inhalation, exhalation, and retention both ways;
The Science of Breath thus consisting – they know not.
They who know the Science of Breath
Are destined to spurn the god of death.
Tirumundirum 571

During deep meditation the breath naturally becomes suspended for a short period of time, and during this interval, there is no sense of time; the mind is still, and in that deep peace, there is joy or bliss. The *yogic* explanation of this phenomenon is that it is the breath (or the movement of *prana*) that enables your mind to think. When this is suspended, then the mind loses its fuel, and so it is no longer distracted, and becomes very still.

Let prana merge in mind
And together the two be stilled
Then no more shall birth and death be
Tirumundirum 567

The stilling of breath is a key parameter in most of the major breathing techniques, and this has led to a lot of controversy on how and when breath retention should be practiced. There are four types of *kumbhaka* or retention of breath mentioned by *Patanjali* in his *Yoga Sutras*:

Bahya kumbhaka [external breath retention]: a pause after a very slow and prolonged exhalation.
Abhyantara kumbhaka [internal breath retention]: a pause after a deep, prolonged inhalation.
Stambha kumbhaka [middle breath retention]: a prolonged pause in between the inhalation and exhalation.
Kevala kumbhaka [spontaneous retention]: this is experienced by the practitioner at any time without any effort. It comes automatically after prolonged practice of *pranayama*.

Although the *Yoga Sutras* does not give any *pranayama* techniques or describe any of the methods of breath retention, some general principles are given:

*The variations in Pranayama are
external, internal or suspended.
The interval is regulated by place, duration and number,
and becomes progressively prolonged and subtle.
The fourth type is the spontaneous suspension
of the breath that occurs while concentrating
on something external or internal.*
Yoga Sutras 2:50,51

In the above *Sutras*, *Patanjali* introduced the factors that can be controlled during the breath retention interval:

Place refers to where the breath is held (external, internal or suspended).
Duration refers to the duration of the breath retention.
Number means the ratio between inhalation, retention and exhalation of the breath.

Hatha Yoga texts, such as the *Hatha Yoga Pradipika* focus primarily on the forceful application of *kumbhaka*, rather than on *kevala*, for the simple reason that there are no specific techniques for *kevala*, and it normally takes prolonged practice to achieve the latter, while the effects of forceful breath retention can be quick. However, the unsupervised and indiscriminate practice of such forced breath retention can be dangerous to the physical and mental health of the practitioner.

*Pranayama can eradicate all diseases if properly practiced,
but if done improperly, may cause aggravation.*
Hatha Yoga Pradipika 2.16

As long as the prana remains in the body,
the soul does not depart.
Therefore, practice pranayama , to prolong life.
Goraksha Shataka 91

The potential life-force hidden in matter,
can be harnessed for liberation
by those who have been empowered,
but brings bondage to the uninitiated.
Gorakhsa Shataka 56

Every authoritative text on pranayama, apparently requires the forced holding of breath. As previously explained, a competent guide, common sense and the correct application of the *bandhas* or muscular locks are essential factors for the success in practicing forced *holding of breath, or kumbhaka*. Such forced holding of breath, is only used as a bridge, or stop-gap, until the practitioner can enter into the effortless state of spontaneous suspension of breath. There can be negative health consequences from such unnecessary exertions. Even in *Hatha Yoga*, the goal of *pranayama* is to achieve the state of *kevala* or spontaneous stilling of breath.

The *pranayama* techniques described in the subsequent sections, do not require forced holding of breath, and in fact, encourages the spontaneous stilling of breath. This ensures that they can be practiced relatively safely, enhancing their health benefits, without diminishing their spiritual effectiveness.

The Benefits of Pranayama

The great *Siddha* or perfected being called *Tirumoolar* has given us the manifold benefits of *pranayama*, in his great text of yoga, called the Tirumandirum:

1. Longevity of the body is gained by breath control

If breath that is forked in and out
Is on mind directed and centered,
Well may you sleep
In the spacious bed chamber,
Of the Body Cave
That has doors two and windows seven
And long, long may you live there too.
Tirumandirum 594

By controlling inhalation and exhalation of the breath, and centering of the mind, the body is preserved. The physical body has nine openings: two eyes, two nostrils, two ears, mouth, genital opening, and anal opening. The nine-windowed house is the vehicle of the soul.

2. The mind is tamed by breath control

If of the ten vayus that fill the body
Five by exhalation leave,
What avails you fool!
What though you wake and pray?
They who control breath in measure ordained,
Will sure imprison mind -monkey
Within the body fortress.
Tirumandirum 595

The mind has been likened by *Swami Vivekenanda*, to a drunken monkey stung by the bee of passion.... almost impossible to tame, and control.

Patanjali has also given emphasize to the benefit of mental control through the breath:

The attainment of Pranayama removes mental darkness and
ignorance, which veils the inner Light of the soul......
And the mind attains the power to concentrate.
Yoga Sutras 2:52-3

When the breath is controlled, the mind becomes still, and concentration or one-pointedness arises.

3. Purification of the Energy and Physical Bodies

The breath is used to flush the ida and pingala
By Pranayama, the heart gets purified,
And the body becomes impervious even to fire.
Tirumandirum 726

The *ida* and *pingala* are two *nadis* or energy channels which transport *prana* or life-force in the Energy Body, analogous to blood vessels which transport oxygen to the organs in the Physical Body. By the purification of the Energy and Physical Bodies, the *prana* or healing life-force can travel unobstructed.

4. Breath control leads to *Samadhi* or the ecstatic state of Yoga

When prana course through the adharas six
Then will nectar be;
When prana reaches the seventh center of the Sun

And further onward to the eighth center of the Moon;
In the ninth center prana attains Samadhi.
Tirumandirum 703

The *adharas* are also called *chakras* or wheels of energy, and are the localized energy centers in the Energy Body. This verse describes the process of *Kundalini Yoga*, when the *Kundalini* or latent potential life-force in the root or 1st *chakra* travels unobstructed to the higher centers.

When you practice *pranayama* effectively, the veil of dark ignorance that covers the inner light is removed. *Pranayama* leads to the removal of the obstacles that distract the mind, so that it becomes easy to concentrate and meditate, which will eventually result in enlightenment and self-realization. This has been stated by the great *Rishi Vasistha*, who was the mentor of the divine incarnation, *Rama*:

The wise ones declare that the mind is caused by
the movement of prana.
By the practice of Pranayama, the mind is stilled.
When the mind ceases its movement,
the world-illusion dissolves [Nirvana]
Yoga Vasistha V. 78.46

Rudra Shivananda

The Yogic Five-Body Model

Refer to Figure 11.

1. The physical body is what most of us identify with. It is the only reality which the majority of humanity recognizes, being composed of blood and bones, the nervous system and sense organs

2. The energy body is just above our normal conscious perception, but can be sensed in recognition of the presence of vitality. It is like an overlay on the physical body energizing and regulating the physical cells. It acts as a channel between the physical world and the higher subtle worlds. Here is where the *chakras* or energy centers are particularly active. Here is also the main focus of the practice of *pranayama*. This energy body is also called the *pranayamakosha*.

3. The emotional body serves as the mediation between the physical and mental bodies, converting the physical vibrations from the neutral sensations into the "emotionally charged sensations" by adding the qualities of "pleasant" or "unpleasant" or encapsulating it with feelings such as desire or fear. Most physical diseases arise from the emotional or energy bodies.

4. The mental body is the abode of knowledge and analytical thinking. The "emotionally charged sensations" from the emotional body is processed into perceptual units and fitted into patterns calling forth responses which vibrate back through the emotional body back into the physical realm, causing a physical reaction. This is the realm of thoughts and habit patterns.

[58]

5. The causal body is both the home of wisdom and of our *karmic* debts. This is the abode of the evolving soul. Higher abstract and intuitive insights arise from here.

Figure 11. The Five-Body Model

The five-body complex exists and functions in different 'dimensions' and each is maintained by a different type of energy, from the physical chemical reactions to the subtlest consciousness energy. Each of the bodies has its own energy centers or *chakras* as well as energy channels for controlling and distributing their own level of energy. Orthodox science only recognizes the centers and channels associated with the physical body, where the cardio-vascular system represents the channels, and the brain and various nerve plexuses correspond to the energy centers. As the *chakras* are activated and awakened, you will become aware of the corresponding dimension of reality, giving you a fuller understanding of the lower dimensions.

Pranamayakosha or Energy Body

The ancient seers have always had the ability to see beyond the physical body, to comprehend the totality of a person's manifestation. Even now, those with the sensitivity, see the aura that surrounds the physical body. This aura that seemingly envelopes the physical body is the appearance of the energy body or *pranamaykosha*, which together with the emotional, mental, and causal "bodies" form what is loosely called the astral body.

Truly, other than the physical sheath,
Which is the essence of food,
Is the vital body,
The exact form and shape of the person
Taittiriyopanisad II.2

The *Chakras or energy centers*

It has been pointed out in ancient *yogic* texts, that *yogis* are those who truly know the *chakras* or Energy Centers. This exemplifies how critical and potentially complex this whole topic can become.

These Energy Centers cannot be found by dissecting the physical body, but only through achieving higher states of consciousness. Figure 12 gives the location of the *chakras* in relation to the physical body. They are called wheels because of the circular movement of the energies that whirl in and out of them. They are also visualized as lotuses, as shown in figure 13.

These Energy Centers are affected by changes in our internal states, as well as by external vibrations, such as thoughts, words, or actions of others. In the average person, these Centers are functioning sub-optimally, and are not harmonized with each other. As the health of the person is decreased through pollution and tension, the more out of tune these Centers become.

Center 1 [*Muladhara*]: This is also called the Root Center, and is located at the base of the spine in the perineum and is the root and support of all the other centers. It is connected with the subtle element "earth" representing solidity, and therefore is closely related to the physical body.

Center 2 [*Swadhisthana*]: This is located two inches above the 1st Center along the spine, and is associated with the subtle element water, representing fluidity and movement. This is the center for the emotional body.

Center 3 [*Manipura*]: This is located at the level of the navel, and is associated with the subtle element fire, representing transformation of energy. This center is closely related to the energy body.

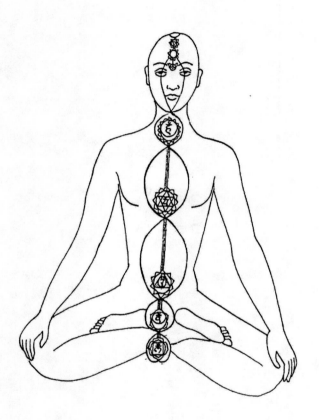

Figure 12. The chakras in the Energy Body

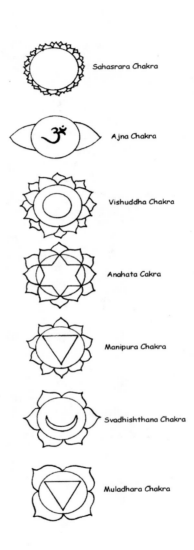

Figure 13. The popular forms of the chakras

Center 4 [*Anahata*]: This is located at the spine at the heart level and is associated with the subtle element air, representing the mind and is the center of the mental body.

> *The soul is restless until one realizes the essence of*
> *the twelve-petalled lotus of the heart,*
> *attaining freedom from merits and demerits.*
> Goraksha Shataka 24

Center 5 [*Vishuddhi*]: This is located at the throat and is associated with the subtle element ether, representing consciousness. This is the center for the causal or spiritual body, and is considered the seat of the soul.

Center 6 [*Ajna*]: This is located in the center of the head at the level just above the eyes, traditionally called the "third eye" and is the center for superconsciousness.

Center 7 [*Sahasrara*]: This is located at the crown of the head and is associated with the Absolute or Transcendent Reality.

PRANA, the Vital Energy of the Universe

Prana, as fire burns
Prana, as the sun shines
Prana, as the clouds rains
Prana, as the lord of gods, rules
Prana is the earth, the moon, the shining ones
Prana is both form and formless
Prasnopanisad 2:5

The Sanskrit word *prana* is usually translated as 'first unit of life-force'. There are many terms used for it, including 'vital energy', 'breath of life' and 'life-force.' *Paramahansa Yogananda* translated it as 'lifetrons,' in essence, condensed thoughts of God or substance of the astral world.

When there is prana in the body, it is called life
When prana leaves the body, it results in death.
Hatha Yoga Pradipika 2:3

Prana is the link between the astral and physical bodies. When this link is broken or cut off, then the astral body separates from the physical body, and what we call death takes place. The *prana* departs from the physical body and is withdrawn into the astral body. It is not the oxygen in the breath that determines life and death. No amount of oxygen will keep a person from the departure of life from its body – it is the life-force, the "living and intelligent energy" of *prana*.

All living beings, whether human, plants or minerals, are dependent on some amount of life bestowing *prana*.

When the breath is restless,
the mind also becomes unsteady

Rudra Shivananda

When the breath is still,
so is the activity of the mind
Therefore restrain one's breath
to attain a motionless consciousness
Hatha Yoga Pradipika 2:2

When you become more aware of your state of mind and of the emotions such as anger, fear, hatred and jealousy, you can begin to feel what effect it has on your breathing. When you become angry or emotionally upset, your breathing is markedly changed in its rate and depth. When you become angry, the breath becomes faster and there is lose of control over it and over the mind. The emotions and the mental processes are related to the nervous system and through it they change the breathing pattern. That is why it is important to develop positive attitudes and positive thoughts, and to change or overcome unwanted negative or destructive tendencies and behaviors.

Prana is intimately related to the mind and mental processes, such that when there is disturbance in the mind, the breath becomes restless and vice versa – the movement of *prana* also affects the mind and its mental processes. When the mind expresses positive attitudes, then the energy or *prana* moves in an upward flow, permeating the whole body and elevating the consciousness. Conversely, if we become negative in our thoughts, attitudes and behavior, the *prana* flows downward, and the energy becomes concentrated in the lower part of the body causing depression or agitation.

The Ten Vayus or Life-forces of the Body

Once *prana* enters the physical body through the vehicle of the breath, it takes on certain differentiated functions and become localized near certain major parts of the body, and move intelligently as required. The differentiated *pranas* are called *vayus* (vital airs) and there are ten of them in our "energy body". The five major *vayus* function through the five subsidiary nerve centers in the brain and spinal cord.

The Five Major Vayus

Udana vayu functions in the body between the larynx and the top of the head. It controls speech, the sense of balance, memory and intellect. *Udana* has an upward movement – it carries *kundalini*[the potential energy for self-realization] to the crown or seventh energy center, *sahasrara*. It separates the astral body and physical body at the time of death. *Udana* is pale white in color.

Prana vayu functions in the region between the larynx and base of the heart. It controls speech, the respiratory muscles, blood circulation and body temperature. *Prana* is the color of coral.

Samana vayu functions between the heart and the navel region, maintaining a balance between *apana* and *prana*. It controls all the metabolic activity involved in digestion. *Samana* is translucent milky white.

Apana vayu functions in the region from the navel to the feet. It normally has a downward movement, but under certain circumstances will carry the *kundalini* upwards in *Sushumna* [the central *nadi* or energy channel coincident with the spinal cord] to unite with *prana*. This *apana* controls the functions of the kidneys, excretory system, colon, rectum and sex organs and is pink in color.

Rudra Shivananda

Vyana vayu permeates throughout the whole body and is an aura around the body. It helps the other *vayus* to function properly. Specifically, it controls both the voluntary and involuntary movements of the muscles and joints, keeps the whole body upright by generating unconscious reflexes along the spine, as well as controlling the physical nerves and the *nadis* or subtle astral/energy channels. *Vyana* is the color of a ray of sunlight.

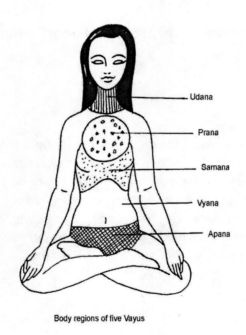

Body regions of five Vayus

Figure 14. The Five major pranas

The Five Minor Pranas

Naga vayu controls the function of belching and hiccoughing and contributes to consciousness.

Kurma vayu controls the function of opening the eyelids and causes vision.

Karikara vayu controls sneezing and induces hunger and thirst.

Devadatha vayu controls yawning.

Dhananjaya vayu causes the decomposition of the body after death.

Prana always lies in the chest, apana in the lower regions,
samana is in the region between the chest and navel,
udana moves in the throat, while vyana pervades the body.
Naga is the minor prana for belching,
kurma for winking, karikara for sneezing, and
devadatta for yawning. Dhananjaya pervades the
whole body and functions after the soul leaves.
Goraksha Shataka 34, 35, 36, 37

Rudra Shivananda

The Mind – Breath Connection

> *Yoga is the cessation of identifying with the*
> *vrittis [fluctuations] arising within consciousness.*
> *Yoga Sutras I.2*

The aim of *pranayama* is self-realization through controlling the mind and suspending the mental fluctuations or *vrittis*. With the breath calm and mind still, the inner light of the true Self shines radiantly.

Vrittis are caused by instincts, urges and desires

Vrittis can be translated as 'fluctuations', 'modifications of the mind', and 'thought-waves'.

In order to understand these mental fluctuations, we must first examine the mind which exists in the mental body [what is commonly called the astral body is made up of four components, one of which is the mental component]. It contains four main elements:

Manas (mind): responsible for thinking, willing, doubting, and recording faculty of the mind

Buddhi (intellect): the intuitive wisdom, discriminating and decision-making faculty of the mind

Ahamkara (ego): individuation faculty and identifying faculty of mind

Chitta (consciousness): storehouse of past experiences; memory; 'mind-stuff', mental substratum

The *chitta* or 'mind-stuff' is a composite of three primordial energies or attributes of *prakriti* [nature] called *gunas* or qualities:

>*Sattva* – quality of truth, purity, light
>*Rajas* – quality of passion, desire, energy
>*Tamas* – quality of ignorance, darkness, inertia

The *gunas* interact constantly with each other, and at any moment, one is predominant:

>When the mind has a dominant *sattvic* quality, it performs good actions, it is virtuous, peaceful, calm joyful and selfless.

>When the mind has a *rajasic* nature it is egotistical, absorbed in worldly and selfish interests. It is restless with desires.

>When the mind is being dominated by the quality of *tamas*, it is dull, negative, careless, ignorant, lethargic, depressive.

Chitta is like a lake on which the *vrittis* or waves, rise and fall, by the interaction of the three *gunas*, These waves are the innumerable thoughts that give existence to the mind. Without these *vrittis* or 'thought-waves', the mind has no separate existence. The mind clings to these thoughts and identifies with them, and therefore "thinks", feels and directs the senses to act accordingly.

The *ahamkara* or ego-sense, through its "I-ness", gives the motive power to the instinctual tendencies in the mind, generating desires relative to objects through an outward projection, and accepts them inwardly as memory.

According to *Patanjali*, the innumerable vrittis that are rising and falling in each moment within the *chitta* or mental lake can be divided into five main categories, called *kleshas* (afflictions). *Kleshas* are of two kinds:

> *Klishta* (afflicted, painful, distressing)
> *Akilishta* (not afflicted; non-painful, pleasing)

These *kleshas* are the five main causes of suffering in life which has been identified by *Patanjali* in his *Yoga Sutras*, II:3-9:

> *Avidya* or ignorance
> *Asmita* or I-am-ness
> *Raga* or attraction
> *Dvesha* or aversion
> *Abhinivesha* or fear of death

The source of all other obstacles is *avidya* or ignorance. *Avidya* is the ignorance of our spiritual identity as the eternal and blissful Self. Ignorance creates delusion, which covers the knowledge of the Self. Without experiencing our own true divine nature, we cannot realize that this same immortal Self exists in all creatures. In ignorance we create a sense of separation from the Divine and from each other.

Asmita is identification of the Self with the body, mind and senses. It is the forgetfulness of our true divine nature, and the assumption of the false-amour of ego-sense, by which we experience ourselves as finite, limited and temporal.

Raga is the restless pursuit of pleasure, and attraction to the objects of the senses. It is also a confusion of wants and needs.

Dvesha is a dislike or avoidance of that which brings unhappiness and suffering.

The fifth *klesha, abhinivesha,* is the tenacious clinging to life, not wanting to let go of the ego. It also manifests as the resistance to change. This is the habit of dependence on objective sources for enjoyment and happiness, and the fear of losing them. The greatest fear is the fear of death, the fear that we will cease to exist and lose our identity.

Patanjali has also given us the remedy for overcoming these five *kleshas* or afflictions in *Yoga Sutras* II:10-11. He informs us that these afflictions may be subtle or gross. The gross, active and outward expressions of the five afflictions can be eliminated through self-discipline and meditation. The subtle afflictions can be dissolved by reversal or purification of the energy of the thought responsible for each affliction. For example, if the feeling of attraction or repulsion enters the mind, then substitute it with contentment and acceptance, respectively.

According to *Patanjali* (*Yoga Sutras* II:26), the best anti-dote for ignorance is the unwavering practice of uninterrupted awareness, discriminating between that which is real, and that which is unreal. Self-realization is attained by discrimination, dispassion, determination, unbroken awareness, whole-hearted dedication to the practice of *Yoga* and meditation. It takes patience and perseverance to still the mind by the practice of *pranayama*.

The Nadis

The *nadis* are a network of energy channels situated throughout the *pranamayakosha* [Energy Body]. The two primary nourishing *nadis* are the *ida* and the *pingala*. The *ida* and the *pingala* are situated on the left and right sides of the physical spinal cord. The vital life-force, *prana*, flows through these energy channels or tubes. In between these two *nadis* is the *sushumna nadi*, which is the most significant of all the energy tubes. The *sushumna nadi* is the central channel into which the yogi tries to direct the *prana* to flow, so as to stimulate and awaken the *kundalini*, or primordial potential energy for self-realization.

Throughout the subtle or energy body there are about 72,000 *nadis* which circulate *prana* throughout the body. In the Brihadaranyaka Upanishad, a *vedic* scripture, which is one of the oldest of the Upanishads, dating from before 800 B.C.E., it says that the *nadis* are as fine as a hair split 1,000 times.

The source of the three major nadis is an egg-shaped area called *kanda*, that is located between the anus and the root of the genitals. This is also the junction of the *sushumna* and the first or root *chakra*, called the *muladhara chakra*. From the *kanda*, the *nadis* distribute *prana* all over the body.

Ida, pingala, and sushumna, are always conductors
of the prana, and are connected. Their presiding powers
are the moon, sun, and fire respectively.
Goraksha Shataka 32

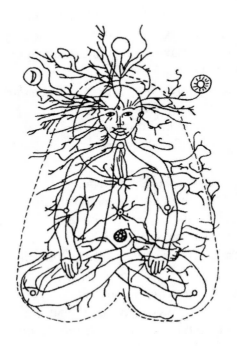

Figure 15. The system of Nadis

Kundalini Shakti

Kundalini is the nascent potential energy, frozen and locked away in the physical-energetic-emotional-mental body complex, inhabited by the spiritual light of the soul.

It is the microcosmic counterpart to the macrocosmic energy paradigm, called *Shakti*. This all-encompassing *Shakti*, is the creative matrix of the universe, as well as, the Universal life-force energy – the Universal *Prana*. Each body-mind-soul complex is enervated by an aspect of the Universal *Prana*, the individual *prana*, forming the five major *vayus*, and five minor *vayus*, distributed through the *nadi* system.

Prana in the body is the lowest layer of the *Kundalini Shakti*. This lowest level is always active in the human body, for it is the basis of life itself. When, by diligent practice of *pranayama*, the higher layers are awakened and activated, there is a quantum leap in evolution, with the concomitant raising of consciousness. This process is commonly called *Kundalini* Awakening, or the raising of *Kundalini*.

The concept of raising the *Kundalini* is based on the model of *Kundalini* being situated in the 1st Energy Center or *muladhara chakra*. When the *Kundalini* is awakened, it rises up the central channel, the *sushumna nadi*. By diligent practice, it is raised from one energy center to the next, until it reaches the seventh, the crown center. A *yogi* is one who has raised the *Kundalini* to the 7th Energy Center, the thousand-petalled lotus, and consequently achieved self-realization, attaining the highest potential of soul evolution.

However, it is necessary to humbly remind oneself, that raising the second level of *Kundalini*, a work of many life-times, is not the end of the cosmic evolutionary journey. Other layers await to be conquered in higher realms. Rare as the birth of a galaxy, is one who rises even to the third level on this earth.

There have been many misrepresentations about *Kundalini*, especially in recent times, because of the preference for mental speculation, over real practice. Such fantasies by unqualified writers and those who have not perfected their practice, have stoked the fires of fear and doubt.

Some people have misunderstood the ancient texts, and claim that a great *yogic* sage, *Yagnavalkya*, taught that *Kundalini* should not be awakened, but rather removed, as she was a blockage to the attainment of the *samadhi* state of consciousness, or ecstatic spiritual realization.

Another popular myth is that of *Kundalini* Psychosis, supposedly referring to the physical, emotional and mental disorders that occur when *Kundalini* rises prematurely or does not enter the central channel, but wanders elsewhere.

What is called *Kundalini* Psychosis, is more aptly called *pranic* disorder of the Nervous System. The wisdom of those who have the right to speak on such matters, the Masters of *Yoga*, declares that *Kundalini* will not arise prematurely – She is an intelligent force, which will only rise up when the aspirant is ready and She will not go into other energy channels, except for the central channel, or *sushumna*.

So, what is going on? Something serious is happening, and we are not trying to minimize the life disruptions documented. In reality, it is the *prana* or life-force energy which is responsible. Just as a frayed or flawed electric wire gets "fried", when a higher current is passed through it, just so, when an excessive amount of *prana* is passed through a damaged or flawed Energy Body, negative reactions occur.

How is it possible for the Energy Body to be damaged? The physical nervous system can become damaged through the overuse of drugs, or accidents. Such damage gives rise to concurrent damage in the Energy Body. For their own safety, those with such problems, should not practice *pranayama*, or be in the presence of higher energy levels, such as power centers, or Masters who transmit *prana*.

The only solution for such *pranic* disturbances, is to repair the physical damage, and/or stop the use of drugs. The last thing those suffering from such disorders, should do, is to excercerbate their condition with *pranic* practices. It may take many years, for the normal process of healing to occur. For those few, who can find a living Master of Breath, capable and willing to help, repairing of the Energy Body can be done quicker and safely.

The Kundalini is drawn upward, through
the sushumna, like a thread through a needle,
by the mind, aroused through the
union of fire and prana.
As one must apply pressure to open
a door with a key, so the yogi opens the
door to liberation by Kundalini.
Goraksha Shataka 49, 51

Ashtanga Yoga

The practice of *pranayama* must be understood by placing it within the perspective of the overall system of *yoga*. It is not practiced in a vacuum, but in relationship to various other disciplines.

Pranayama has been integrated into various spiritual schools, but the one that is primarily taught by the *Naths* and *Siddhas*, is the one mentioned by *Patanjali*, commonly called *Ashtanga Yoga*, by others, because of the eight parts or branches of the system:

*Self-restraint, fixed observances, postures, breath expansion,
internalization, concentration, contemplation, union with the
Divine, are the eight parts of Yoga*
Yoga Sutras II.29

Patanjali himself did not use the term *Ashtanga*, but actually called his system *Kriya Yoga*, but did not elaborate on its details. However, it may be surmised that the eight limbs mentioned by him, must be necessary aspects of it.

Without the proper practice of breath expansion and control, the rest of the system will not work. Oral tradition states that without *pranayama*, the other parts or limbs of *yoga*, cannot be effectively practiced. Therefore, *pranayama* must be integrated into all the other parts. It is also said by the wise, that by practicing *pranayama*, all the other facets of Yoga will be revealed and attained, in due time.

Nonetheless, for the attainment of higher states of consciousness, and eventually Self-Realization, it is helpful to complement the *pranayama* practice with some, if not all the other parts of the system. Especially useful are the practice of *yamas*, *niyamas*, and the understanding of *pratyahara.*

Self-Restraint : the taming of the Mind

Self-Restraint (*yama*) in *yoga* practice is not only a moral or ethical injunction, as in a religious context, but serves very practical and important functions in enabling the goal of spiritual evolution towards self-realization. By the yogic practice of Self-restraint, the practitioner's mind is tamed and becomes a conduit for the unfettered experience of higher consciousness, from the Divine, the True Self.

> *Yoga is the cessation [of identifying with] the fluctuations*
> *[arising within] consciousness.*
> *Then the seer abides in his own true nature.*
> *Patanjali's Yoga Sutras: 1.2-1.3*

> *The restraints are non-violence, truthfulness, non-stealing,*
> *chastity, and greedlessness.*
> *Yoga Sutras: 2.30*

It is important to understand that the *yamas* are interrelated with one another, and also with the *niyamas*, or disciplined observances. For example, the *niyama* contentment [*santosha*] will protect one from stealing. Besides, meaning 'restraint', *yama* is also the name of the King of Death, which calls to mind that there must be a dying to ignorance, which is the source of egoism, attachment and repulsion.

By practicing these restraints, the subtle body, with its energy channels are purified, enabling more energy and life-force to flow through them, as well as to ease the upward movement of the *kundalini* through the *chakras*.

We are all beset with obstacles and problems as we turn towards the divine, to reach our highest potential. It is necessary to be constantly examining your thoughts, words and actions with awareness and discrimination - you will then come to an understanding of why problems and obstacles occur, and by which means they can be avoided. By turning the attention within (Self-awareness) to observe the inner obstacles, thoughts and feelings, the obstructions will be revealed. You will realize what agitates the mind and veils the truth. The *yamas* are to be practiced in thought, word and deed, for example, negative thoughts, harsh words, and physical hurt are all lack of restraint of non-violence or *ahimsa*.

Ahimsa: Non-harming, Non-violence, Non-injury

In the state of divine union, *Samadhi*, the yogic sages have unanimously stated that all life is one. If we are to achieve that realization, we must affirm that oneness and unity by being kind, compassionate and respectful to all living beings in thought, word and actions.

We are advised to refrain from causing or wishing harm, distress or pain to any living being, including ourselves and the world we live in. It would also be necessary to dissuade others from harmful or violent actions - it is not enough to just avoid violence. We should not only refrain from violence against living beings, but in all its manifestations – there can be violence in the way you close a door, cut someone off on the freeway, or even call out a name.

Ahimsa is not merely non-killing or 'Thou shalt not kill'. To live in ahimsa, it is important to develop an attitude of perfect harmlessness with positive love and respect for all life, not just in our actions, but in our thoughts and words as well. With perfection of *ahimsa* one realizes the unity and oneness of all life and attains universal love, peace and harmony. With perfect practice of ahimsa one rises above anger, hatred, fear, envy and attachment.

Satya: Non-lying, Truthfulness

Truth or *Sat* is one of the aspects of the Divine. As our essential nature is this same Divinity, it is against our true nature to exaggerate, pretend, distort or lie to others, or to manipulate people for our own selfish concerns. When we live in truthfulness we become anchored in the awareness of the Divine.

Why do we lie? It is because of selfishness and the fear of losing one's reputation. However, you can fool some of the people some of the time, but you can never fool your true Self, anytime! Honesty with oneself is the first step towards self-improvement.

Can someone achieve any self-realization or self-knowledge by lying to others and oneself? If you tell lies, you build up a personality, which consists of lies and you deceive yourself. If you are immersed in lying, you will never know the truth or the Divine.

Asteya: Non-stealing

The primary cause for people stealing is the lack of contentment, which leads to greed and desire, manifesting as insecurity, selfishness, greed, and poverty consciousness.

When we are discontent with the present, desire keeps one continually looking to the future for one's fulfillment, instead of realizing that perfection is attainable here and now. To try to gain satisfaction, by fulfilling the endless desires, that arise in the mind, is an utterly futile endeavor, which only cause unhappiness and sorrow. Desire arises from the ego or "I" consciousness, from the thoughts of 'I want', 'I need', or 'I must have'.

In the experience of the great sages, contentment arises only from permanent happiness and joy, permanent peace, and love, and not in the satisfaction of passing desires. To experience this we must look within, it cannot be found outside of ourselves.

Brahmacharya: Non-sensuality, Chastity

Brahmacharya is consciousness anchored in the Divine. It is mind ever turned toward the Divine. It is the state of Yoga or ecstatic union with the Source of All. In *Yoga, brahmacharya* becomes effortless. However, until *Yoga* is achieved, continuous effort is necessary to turn our thoughts, words and actions towards the Divine.

In ancient India, most saints and yogis were householders.They would bring up families, performing their duties to society, while continuing their practice of yoga and leading a spiritual life. To them, there was no conflict between sex and God. Asceticism and celibacy were only temporary periods of intense practice.

Aparigraha: Non-attachment, Non-greed

The Sanskrit word *apara* means 'of another' and *agraha* to 'crave for'. Therefore, *aparigraha* is usually translated as 'without craving for that which belongs to another.' However, in a deeper sense, it means not to be craving for the "unreal", the "not-self" – it is non-attachment to everything that is not the True Self.

Non-greed, in this context, is not only resisting the temptation to covet what belongs to others, but also means non-attachment even to one's own possessions, as well as not to hoard or accumulate unnecessary amounts of something.

Unsteadiness of the mind or restlessness is an obstacle to spiritual progress. In his Yoga Sutras (2:3), Patanjali lists five afflictions that disturb mental equilibrium: ignorance, egoism, attraction to pleasure and aversion to pain, and clinging to life. Of these five afflictions, ignorance (*avidya*) is the source of all the other obstacles. Ignorance leads to a mistaken sense of duality, which gives rise to a desire to experience, from which egoism or "I-sense" takes root. The ego principle gives rise to greed and insecurity

Niyamas

The five *niyamas* are purity [*saucha*], contentment [*santosha*], austerity [*tapas*], self-study [*swadhyaya*], and surrender to the Divine [*Iswara pranidhana*].

These positive observances, exercise the physical, emotional, mental and spiritual 'muscles' promoting strength in all these aspects of our being. Habitual negative patterns are re-aligned, minimized, and eliminated by the practice of the *niyamas*. The personality is re-organized for the enfoldment of higher consciousness.

Saucha

There is both purity of body and mind. It is relatively easy to maintain a clean physical body. The practices of positive thinking, mindfulness and intellectual discrimination produce purity of the mind. Mental purity is necessary for successful inward examination and concentration, leading to the development of self-knowledge. In the absence of physical cleanliness, one is more susceptible to germs, while the absence of mental purity makes one more susceptible to emotional disturbances and psychosomatic illnesses.

Santosha

Contentment is the non-attachment to all physical, emotional and mental pleasures and possessions. It is also the offering of the results from all actions to the Divine, performing selfless action, in the service of humanity.

Tapas

This is the practice of austerity for the purpose of generating spiritual heat and the light of Super-consciousness. It is not self-mortification and physical torture, as many have misinterpreted.

The practice of *pranayama*, which generates heat and light, is *tapas*.

Swadhyaya

This includes all types of self-study that lead to increase in self-knowledge and self-understanding. Outwardly, one should study the scriptures and learn from great saints and sages. Such activities require discrimination, as there are often superficial conflicts between these diverse sources. Study and assimilation, therefore need to be selectively undertaken, to prevent confusion, in the mind of the student. Inwardly, *swadhyaya* is meditating on the Self.

Pratyahara

It is through the five senses of sight, hearing, taste, smell and touch, that the mind makes contact with the external world. This interaction is a mental disturbance. By withdrawing from the senses, the practitioner begins to function with a less disturbed mind.

A higher degree of concentration of energy and mind is achieved, when they are not dissipated through the senses on external objects.

The practice of *pranayama* will lead to *pratyahara*.

Rudra Shivananda

Clearing some misconceptions about Pranayama

1. It is not necessary to have mastered the first three parts of the Ashtanga [Eight-part] *Yoga*, that is, *yama* [restraints], *niyama* [observances], and *asana* [physical postures], before practicing the fourth part, *pranayama*. There are those who consider that the eight parts of *Yoga* are like the rungs of a ladder, with the higher steps being tread on, only after the lower ones have been transcended. An equally acceptable interpretation is that the eight parts form a whole, and the parts should be practiced together as far as possible. In fact, the effective practice of *pranayama* leads to *pratyahara* [sense-withdrawal], which leads to *dharana* [concentration], merging into *dhyana* [meditation], and finally *samadhi*. There is, of course, the practical matter that the ability to sit firmly for more than an hour, that is, a stable asana, is required for the deeper aspects of *pranayama*.

2. The belief that the forced holding of breath is necessary to practice *pranayama*, is an error. The goal of *pranayama* is the effortless breath retention or *kevala*. There are numerous breath control techniques which do not require forced holding of breath, and even for the few techniques which are taught with forced breath retention, sensible guidance and precautions, should be observed, to prevent physical and mental harm to the practitioner.

3. There is a misconception that the practice of *pranayama* is dangerous, and should be avoided. There are those who teach that meditation is safer. It is not difficult to realize, for those who have made the sincere attempt, that taming the mind is as difficult and dangerous as taming a wild tiger. Taming the breath can be dangerous, but if practiced under proper guidance, it is a very effective method to tame the mind.

[86]

Postures or Asanas for Pranayama

Unless otherwise instructed in the exercises themselves, there are four postures recommended for comfortable and stable sitting – they are *sukhasana, siddhasana, padmasana,* and *vajrasana.* The choice is based on your individual preference and capability.

The physical discipline of sitting correctly is itself of great benefit for the energy system, as well as enhancing mental discipline and improving the powers of concentration.

The four postures that can be used, as shown in figures 16, 17, 18 and 19:

1. *Sukhasana* or 'easy pose' is a cross-legged posture that is the customary relaxed sitting posture on the floor. You may wish to sit on a cushion so as to elevate your pelvis above your legs to decrease the pressure on the legs.

Figure 16. Sukhasana

2. *Siddhasana* or 'perfect pose' is the yogic meditation posture that is highly recommended, for awakening *Kundalini* during *pranayama*. Sit with your legs stretched forward. Bend your left leg and place the heel of the left foot against the perineum.

Figure 17. Siddhasana

Bend your right leg over the left and place it on the left thigh with the right heel resting against the genitals. The knees should be touching the floor.

3. *Padmasana* or the 'lotus posture' has great benefits, if you can get into it without too much strain. Extend both legs forward and bend your right leg carefully over the left, placing it on the left thigh, as close to the groin as possible. Bend your left leg at the knee and place the left foot on the right thigh. It will take some practice to be able to get into and stay in this posture comfortably. A modified and simpler posture is called

the half-lotus, where the left leg is simply tucked in under the right.

Figure 18. Padmasana

4.   *Vajrasana* or 'kneeling pose'. Sit in a kneeling position, with head, neck and trunk straight. It is also possible to put a cushion or stool between the seat and the legs, to reduce the pressure on the feet.

Figure 19 Vajrasana

Another consideration during the practice is the position of the hands and arms. There are three simple positions that can be used with any of the four postures:

1. Open receptive: Rest your hands on your knees with the palms facing up.

2. Place the back of your right hand on top of your left palm with the thumbs lightly touching each other.

3. Interlace your fingers together and rest them on your lap.

Whichever variation and combination of posture and hand position you adopt, it is important to remember not to press your arms into the body, and to relax your shoulders and chest, keeping the head and neck upright and steady.

Additional points to observe for good posture:

1. The back is straight without undue strain, so that energy can flow freely.

2. The shoulders are relaxed and not hunched forward or bent backwards.

3. The mouth should be relaxed and slightly smiling.

4. The eyes are closed but relaxed.

5. The head should be held erect without tension with the neck tucked in ever so gently.

Guidelines for the Practice of Pranayama

Place

Select a peaceful, clean, warm, airy place where you can sit without disturbance by noise, family members, or visitors. It can be a special room, or a dedicated part of a room, or even a garden.

Time

Traditionally, it is recommended that *pranayama* training be best started in spring. However, if you need to start the training, anytime is a good time.

Pranayama can be practiced throughout the year, but do not practice in the heat of the sun or when the body is cold or ill. Just before or during sunrise and after sunset are excellent times for practice.

Posture

The posture you sit in should allow you to keep your back erect from the base of the spine to the neck and you should be able to sit comfortably and relaxed with your eyes closed.

A folded blanket or cushion can be used to lessen the strain. *asanas* recommended for *pranayama* are *sukhasana* (easy pose), *siddhasana* (perfected pose), and *padmasana* (lotus pose).

Precautions

Do not practice *pranayama* immediately after meals. Wait at least three hours after eating. If you are hungry, just eat a small snack or drink. You can eat fifteen minutes after *pranayama*.

Do not force or strain the breath. Avoid jerky movements. Do not struggle to restrain the breath after inhalation or exhalation. If you feel any negative effects, then stop your practice immediately and rest. Use your common sense.

Pregnant women should avoid *kapalabhati* and *bhastrika* (bellows breath) or any techniques involving breath retention during pregnancy. Techniques such as *nadi shuddhi* (alternate nostril breathing), *surya bhedana, chandra bhedana, viloma pranayama* and *ujjayi pranayama* can be beneficially practiced.

Start out by practicing for no more than thirty minutes, to ensure there is no strain and fatigue. One of the goals of *pranayama* is to increase energy, and decrease stress. Slowly, over months, you may extend the time to one hour, or more.

Be regular in your practice. It is more beneficial to practice a little everyday, than it is to practice a lot for a few days and then stop for a few days, before resuming.

Warm-up and Preparation

Before commencing *pranayama* practice, it is good to do a few preliminary warm-up exercises to open the chest and lungs to facilitate good breathing. A set of warm-up 'Yogic Energization' exercises has been given in Part 1. In addition, the following is a useful exercise for the lungs.

Warm-up

Stand with your feet together and your arms by your sides. Slowly take a long, deep inhalation as you slowly raise your arms above your head, stretch right up onto your toes and pull your shoulders back as you stretch your arms up above your head. Then as you exhale, slowly lower your arms back down to your sides. Repeat five times.

Stand with the feet hip-width apart and inhale as you raise your arms above your head. Keep your arms straight, but with your hands and wrist relaxed. Exhale as you rotate your arms forward in a wide circle. Inhale as you raise your hands and exhale as you lower them. Practice the forward motion of the arms for five rounds then change direction and rotate them back in a reverse motion.

Preparation

Exercise 1: Nostril opening and balancing

This helps to open up both nostrils, as usually one will be blocked. [To learn more about this, refer to Part 3]. Sit on your knees, or otherwise comfortably, with your back straight. Cross your arms and place your hands underneath your armpits, with the thumbs pointing upwards. With a little pressure, press both arm-pits on your hands. Close your eyes and concentrate on the point between the eyebrows. Breathe slowly and rhythmically, with awareness on the breath.

Rudra Shivananda

As a preparation for *pranayama*, this posture can be held for 1-3 minutes. As a standalone exercise, it can be practiced at any time, even after meals. It keeps both nostrils open, relieving discomfort from blocked nasal passages. For maximum benefit, it should be held for at least ten minutes.

Exercise 2: Complete Cleansing Breath

This breath is very beneficial for ventilating and cleansing the lungs. It stimulates the cells and gives a good tone to the respiratory organs. It also eliminates carbon dioxide from the system.

Caution: This exercise should not be practiced by those with heart problems or with abnormal blood pressure.

1. Standing position:
   Stand with your feet shoulder width apart, arms relaxed by your sides. Take a complete *Yogic* breath, and raise your hands over your head. Then with your lips puckered, exhale the breath out powerfully making a 'whoosh' sound, as you slowly bend at the knees to bring your hands between your knees and towards the floor. Slowly inhale through your nostrils as you rise up and bring the hands overhead again. Perform this three times.

2. Sitting position:
   Sit comfortably in one of the recommended postures. Place your hands on your knees. Inhale a complete *Yogic* breath. Then pucker your lips and exhale vigorously through them in a series of short, sharp exhalations as you slowly lower your trunk and forehead as close to the floor as possible.

Then slowly raise your head and trunk back up while slowly breathing in through the nostrils. Perform this three times.

3. Alternate nostril cleansing:
    Sit in a comfortable posture with your spine straight and your body relaxed.

    Slowly inhale through both nostrils, then pucker your lips and exhale all the air from your lungs with a series of dynamic exhalations, like a bellows action.

    Closing the right nostril with your right thumb, inhale through the left nostril.

    Then close your left nostril with the third finger of your right hand and exhale through your right nostril, with a series of short, sharp exhalation.

    Continue with inhaling through the right nostril, and exhaling through the left. Start the cycle again with inhaling through both nostrils.

    Practice three rounds.

    This is especially beneficial for those suffering from sinus congestion.

Section A
Life-Force Balancing Pranayama

The Techniques of Pranayama

There may be countless pranayama techniques, but the fourteen practices, and their variations, which are explained, in the following sections are the ones that have been chosen as the most effective. These techniques are usually given one after another in books, without any overall system view. In the oral traditions, there are various ways to group them together, and one system that I prefer is based on their functionality:

1. *Life-force balancing [anuloma-viloma] series*
   -Sukha
   -Purna kosha
   -Chandranuloma viloma
   -Suryanuloma viloma
   -Chandra bheda
   -Surya bheda
   -Nadi shuddhi

2. *Life-force Purification series*
   -Kapalabhati
   -Bhastrika

3. *Life-force expansion series*
   -Ujjayi
   -Sitkari
   -Shitali

4. *Life-force transforming series*
   -Bhramari
   -Murcha

Anuloma-Viloma Pranayama Series

This is the main series of *prana* **balancing** techniques, which should become the basis of your primary practice of *Pranayama*.

The majority of people breathe haphazardly, without concern for the length or strength of the inhalations and exhalations. Neither is there an understanding of the role of the left and right nostrils, in determining the dominance of the right or left brain [more about this subject is given in Part 3]. For our present purposes, it is sufficient to know that, for optimum health of the body-mind complex, a regular, consistent breathing with various ratios between the length of inhalation and exhalation is recommended. Also, a balance between the left and right nostrils during breathing, has profound influence on the integration of the intuitive and analytic brains.

The movement and distribution of the life-force energy, *prana*, is enhanced with these techniques of balancing the inhale/exhale cycle, as well as with the balancing of the left and right nostrils, for the intake of *prana*.

Anuloma means breathing in and *viloma* signifies breathing out. This series is composed of the permutations of breathing in and out with both nostrils, a single nostril, and alternate nostrils.

There are seven techniques in this series:

1. Both nostrils: *sukha pranayama*
2. Both nostrils: *purna kosha pranayama*
3. Left nostril only: *chandranuloma viloma*
4. Right nostril only: *suryanuloma viloma*
5. Alternate nostril 1: *chandra bheda*
6. Alternate nostril 2: *surya bheda*
7. Alternate nostril 3: *nadi shuddhi*

1. Sukha Pranayama or Simple Calming Breath

This is an excellent breathing technique for reducing stress and producing a calm mind. It is considered 'easy', as the name 'sukha', implies, but should not be dismissed, in favor of more complex breathing techniques. This is a case where simplicity does not decrease effectiveness.

Sit comfortably, keeping a smiling face, and relaxed body. Inhale slowly, but without strain from both nostrils, and then exhale slowly through both nostrils.

Feel your body being energized by the breath. Mentally count the duration of the inhalation and try to make the exhalation to be of the same number of counts.

It takes practice to count the duration of your breath, but after a little while, it will be second nature. The key at the beginning is to count consistently, and not vary the speed of the count.

Continue for twelve rounds. After the inhalation or the exhalation, if there is natural pause, don't force the breath, and wait for the continuation. Your respiratory system will take care of it.

It is generally recommended that you begin with a count of six, moving to twelve, after several weeks of practice.

Take the time to learn and practice sukha pranayama. After you are able to perform to a count of twelve, integrate it with the Full Yogic Breath.

The following variations should only be attempted after mastering the basic *sukha pranayama*, or six months of consistent practice. These variations are to help the practitioner gain the spontaneous breathless state. No force should be used.

Variation 1: *Sukha anuloma kevala*

Perform twelve rounds of *sukha pranayama*. On the thirteenth round, after the inhalation, watch the breath, without trying to hold the breath. There may be a moment or longer of time, before the urge to exhale occurs. Exhale to the same count, when the urge to exhale occurs. Practice for a total of seven rounds.

Variation 2: *Sukha viloma kevala*

Perform twelve rounds of *sukha pranayama*. On the thirteenth round, after the exhalation, watch the breath, without trying to hold the breath. There may be a moment or longer of time, before the urge to inhale occurs. Inhale to the same count, when the urge to inhale occurs. Practice for a total of seven rounds.

Variation 3: *Sukha purvaka kevala*

This is a combination of the previous two variations, and should be attempted, only after proficiency in them. Perform twelve rounds of *sukha pranayama*. On the thirteenth round, after the inhalation, watch the breath, without trying to hold the breath. There may be a moment or longer of time, before the urge to exhale occurs. Exhale to the same count, when the urge to exhale occurs. Then watch the breath, and wait for the urge to inhale, to inhale. Practice for a total of seven rounds.

2. *Purna kosha Pranayama*

This *pranayama* utilizes hand *mudras* or psycho-physical gestures to stimulate the physical nervous system, the energetic *nadis*, as well as the emotional, and mental bodies which encompass the human manifestation.

Hand *mudras* for Controlling the Breath

The hand *mudras* covered in this section influence the physical functions of breathing. The *mudras* influence the mind-brain processes and the functions within the nervous system by uniting various nerve terminals of the sympathetic and parasympathetic nervous systems, to influence the respiratory system.

The right lung is divided into three separate compartments or lobes: the lower abdominal lobe, the middle intra-costal lobe and the high clavicular or superior lobe. The left lung has only two lobes: the lower and the higher. A section of the brain controls each of these lung lobes via the nervous system. By applying the hand *mudras* in certain combinations, each lobe can be inflated and deflated independently of one another.

There are five basic hand *mudras*, which have been discovered to influence breathing and therefore the movement of *prana*:

Chinmaya or *jnana mudra*
Make a square by joining together the tip the first finger to the edge of the thumb. The other three fingers are kept outstretched and together. This promotes abdominal breathing.

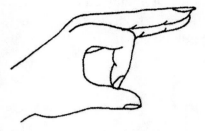

Figure 20. Jnana Mudra

Chin mudra (the symbol of control)
This controls the middle lobes of the lungs and intercostals breathing. Join together the tip of the thumb and the first finger to form a circle. The other three fingers are folded into the palm of the hand, with the tips of the fingers tightly pressed in.

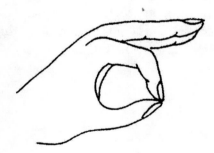

Figure 21. Chin Mudra

Adhi mudra.

This controls the high clavicular breathing. Fold the thumb into your palm and fold the other fingers over the thumb, clenching them into a fist.

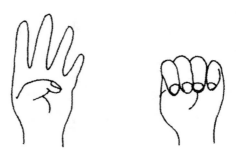

Figure 22. Adhi Mudra

Brahma mudra.

Both hands are clenched into position as in *adhi mudra*, then the knuckles where the fingers join the hand are pressed together, hand to hand, with the fingers turned upwards. The hands in this position are then lowered below the diaphragm, in front of the navel. This controls complete *Yogic* breathing in each of the three parts of the lungs.

Figure 23. Brahma Mudra

Shunya mudra

This *mudra* keeps a lobe of the lung empty while others are being inflated. Open one palm, with the thumb extended at a 90-degree angel to the palm. Make sure the other fingers are extended forward and held tightly together. Place the hand, palm upward, on the junction of the thigh close in to the body.

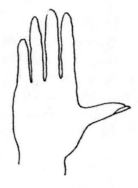

Figure 24. Shunya Mudra

Variation 1

This calms the mind and increases the air intake into the lungs. It harmoniously develops the various parts of the lungs.

Sit in a meditative posture, such as *siddhasana, padmasana* or *vajrasana*. Close your eyes and relax. Place your hands in *chin mudra*, with both hands palms down at the top of your thighs, close to your groin, with the fingers turned inwards. Now inhale and exhale from the abdomen. Practice six rounds of this breath.

Then form *chinmaya mudra*, with both hands at the top of the thighs again. Breathe into the mid-chest lobes of the lungs. Perform six of these intercostal breaths.

Next, position your hands in *adhi mudra* by clenching your fist, with the thumbs inside touching the palms. Place your hands with fingers down on your upper thighs close to the groin. Inhale and exhale six times, into the upper lobes of your lungs, below your collarbones

With your hands still in *adhi mudra*, place both hands together in front of the navel, with the knuckles of each hand pressed together and turned upwards in *brahma mudra*. Now inhale a complete *Yogic* breath, combining the three stages of lower, middle and upper breathing in one long, deep, continuous breath. Then exhale by first emptying out from the lower lungs, then the middle, followed by the upper lungs. Perform this for six rounds

Variation 2

Sit in *vajrasana* or kneeling thunderbolt pose and maintain a relaxed posture with closed eyes.

Place your left hand in *adhi mudra*. The palm should be resting on the top of your left thigh close to your body. Place your right hand in *shunya mudra*, palm upwards on top of the right thigh.

Inhale, with the lobe of the lung on the right side remaining empty, while the left lobe of the lung indicated by the *mudra* of your left hand will inflate and deflate with the respiration. Perform 6 rounds.

Then, reverse the *mudras*, so that you have your left hand in *shunya mudra* and your right hand in *adhi mudra*. Breathe in and out deeply 6 times. You will experience the opposite effect on the left and right lungs.

3. *Chandranuloma viloma Pranayam*

Both the inhalation and exhalation are through the left nostril only. The right nostril is kept closed throughout with the right thumb. The right hand is in *nasik mudra*, in which the first and middle fingers are folded into the palm, the ring and little fingers open, and the thumb closing the right nostril.

Sit in one of the recommended postures, with eyes closed and face relaxed. With the right hand, form the *nasik mudra*, and using the right thumb, close the right nostril.

Inhale smoothly, quietly and as long as you can, through the left nostril.

When you can inhale no further, begin the exhalation smoothly through the left nostril.

This completes one round. Perform fifteen rounds.

This *pranayama* cools the body.

4. *Suryanuloma viloma Pranayama*

Both the inhalation and exhalation are through the right nostril only, keeping the left nostril closed throughout. The right hand is in *nasik mudra*, in which the first and middle fingers are folded into the palm, the thumb open, and the left nostril closed by the ring and little fingers.

Sit in one of the recommended postures, with eyes closed and face relaxed. With the right hand, form the *nasik mudra*, and using the first and middle, close the left nostril.

Inhale smoothly, quietly and as long as you can, through the right nostril.

When you can inhale no further, begin the exhalation smoothly through the right nostril.

This completes one round. Perform fifteen rounds.

This *pranayama* heats up the body.

Figure 25. Nasik Mudra

Rudra Shivananda

5. *Surya bheda Pranayama*

> *Suryabeda prevents old age and death,*
> *and increases the body heat,*
> *awakening the kundalini.*
> Gheranda Samhita 5:62,63

The Sanskrit word *surya* means sun and *bheda* means 'to pierce' or to 'pass through'. *Surya bheda Pranayama* activates the *pingala nadi* or right solar energy channel.

One is cautioned not to practice this technique immediately before or after meals, because it will disturb the energy needed for digestion. Also activating the *pingala nadi* late at night or before going to sleep will keep you awake.

Sit in a meditative posture, preferably *siddhasana* or *padmasana*. Relax and close your eyes and keep a smile on your face.

Variation 1: *without breath retention*

With your right hand in *nasik mudra*, close your left nostril with the ring and little finger. Inhale slowly, quietly, and deeply through the right nostril, keeping your awareness with your breath. As you finish your inhalation, close your right nostril with the thumb, and open the ring and little fingers, exhaling through the left nostril.

This finishes one round, and you begin the second round, by closing the left nostril and inhaling from the right. Therefore, inhalation is always through the right nostril, and exhalation is through the left. Perform 7 rounds.

Variation 2: With kevala

Raise your right hand and place your fingers in *nasik mudra*, as in the previous variation. Close your left nostril with your ring and little fingers. Inhale slowly, deeply, quietly, and with total awareness, through your right nostril.

Observe the breath after the complete inhalation, and when the urge to exhale occurs, then open the left nostril, closing the right nostril with the thumb, and exhaling through the left nostril. This completes one round. Begin the second round by releasing the thumb and closing the left nostril with the ring and little fingers. Perform seven rounds.

6. *Chandra bheda Pranayama*

Chandra means 'moon'. This *pranayama* is basically the same as the Surya bheda except that the inhalations are through the left nostril, and the exhalations through the right.

In this practice the *pranic* life-force is channeled through the *ida* or *chandra nadi*, which cools the body system, whereas the *surya bheda* heats the system.

It is not advisable to practice *surya bheda* and *chandra bheda* on the same day, for they counteract each other's effects.

7. *Nadi shuddhi:* *Alternate Nostril Breathing*

Therefore, learn to direct breath
In streams alternating left and right,
Then shall you taste the nectar of life.
Tirumandirum 567

Nadi shuddhi is the most important *pranayama* for purifying the *nadis* and strengthening the nerves of the physical body. It purifies the blood and the brain cells, and also maintains equilibrium in the catabolic and anabolic processes in the body.

By making the breath flow in each nostril in a balanced way, the *pranic* flow in the *ida* and *pingala nadis* become balanced. Under these balanced conditions, *prana* will flow into the *sushumna* or central *nadi*, awakening the *Kundalini*.

Basic Alternating Breath without forced breath retention

Sit comfortably in *siddhasana, sukhasana,* or *padmasana* with the head, neck and spine in a straight line. Keep a smile on your face and the body relaxed.

Place your left hand on your left knee, relaxed, and form the right hand in *nasik mudra*.

First, exhale through both nostrils, and then close your right nostril with your thumb and inhale slowly and deeply through your left nostril. Close your left nostril with your ring and little fingers, release your thumb and exhale through your right nostril. Inhale through your right nostril, then close it with your thumb and exhale through your left nostril.

This completes one round. Practice only sixteen rounds to begin with, then gradually increase to forty-eight rounds, adding sixteen rounds every week.

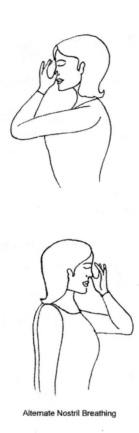

Alternate Nostril Breathing

Figure 25. Basic Alternating Breath

Variation 2: Advanced alternate breathing with kevala

This uses the same alternating breathing pattern as in the previous variation, adding the natural breath retention after the inhalation and before the exhalation.

Sit comfortably in *siddhasana, sukhasana,* or *padmasana* with the head, neck and spine in a straight line. Keep a smile on your face and the body relaxed.

Place your left hand on your left knee, relaxed, and form the right hand in *nasik mudra.*

First, exhale through both nostrils, and then close your right nostril with your thumb and inhale slowly and deeply through your left nostril, counting the length of the inhalation.

Watch your breath, without trying to hold your breath, and wait for the urge to exhale. Then, close your left nostril with your ring and little fingers, release your thumb and exhale through your right nostril, making the exhalation twice as long as the inhalation.

After exhalation is completed, watch your breath, without trying to hold the breath out, and wait for the urge to breath. Then inhale through your right nostril, counting the length of the inhalation. Watch your breath, and wait for the urge to breathe, then close the right nostril with your thumb and exhale through your left nostril, making the exhalation twice as long. Once again, watch the breath, and wait for the urge to breathe, before beginning the inhalation.

This completes one round. Practice only sixteen rounds. Slowly, increase the length of inhalation and exhalation to [16:0:32:0].

Variation 3: Complete alternate breathing

This *pranayama* utilizes a ratio of [16:0:32:0], and the *chakra bija mantras* for the cosmic elements of Air, Fire, Superconsciousness, and Earth.

Sit in the *siddhasana* or *padmasana*, and apply *nasik mudra* for alternating the left and right nostrils.

Be aware of your heart center, and inhale through the left nostril and mentally repeat *yam*, the *bija* or seed *mantra* of the element of Air, for a count of 16 seconds.

Watch your breath, and mentally repeat the *mantra yam*, until you have the urge to breathe. Then, exhale through the right nostril, mentally repeating *yam* 32 times.

Watch your breath, and mentally repeat the *mantra yam*, until you have the urge to breathe.

Now move your awareness to the navel center. Inhale through your right nostril, mentally repeating *ram*, the *bija mantra* of Fire16 times with the breath.

Watch your breath, and mentally repeat the *mantra ram*, until you have the urge to breathe. Then, exhale through the left nostril, mentally repeating *ram* 32 times.

Watch your breath, and mentally repeat the *mantra ram*, until you have the urge to breathe.

Move your awareness to the third-eye center, inside your head, behind the point between the eyebrows. Inhale through your left nostril, mentally repeating *om*, the *bija mantra* of Superconsciousness, 16 times, with the breath.

Watch your breath, and mentally repeat the *mantra om*, until you have the urge to breathe. Then, exhale through the left nostril, mentally repeating *om* 32 times. Watch your breath, and mentally repeat the *mantra om*, until you have the urge to breathe.

Move your awareness to the root center. Inhale through the right nostril, mentally repeating *lam*, the *bija mantra* of Earth, 16 seconds. Repeat the *mantra lam* until you need to breath, then exhale through the left nostril, mentally repeating *lam* 32 times.

Practice a minimum of 3 rounds, moving slowly to 7 rounds, then to 16 rounds.

Section B
Life Force Purification Pranayama

Purification Pranayama Series

Perform exhalation and inhalation rapidly
like the bellows of a blacksmith.
This is called kapalabhati and destroys all mucous problems.
Hatha Yoga Pradipika 2:35

Kapalabhati

Kapalabhati is 'that which brightens the brain', that is, the brain cells are stimulated by this *pranayama*. We usually inhale actively and exhale passively. This technique reverses the active role, so that exhalation is active and inhalation becomes passive. The focus is on abdominal breathing and the abdominal muscles are used to propel the breath out in a series of fast successive bursts. The posture used can be *siddhasana* or *vajrasana* [kneeling pose].

Primary Kapalabhati with both nostrils

Breathe in fully through both nostrils and allow the abdominal muscles to extend slightly. Then pull in the abdominal muscles, and exhale rapidly with a burst of air outward. Allow the abdomen to expand, and let inhalation occur. This is one round.

A minimum of 36 rounds should be practiced, increasing to 144 rounds, by adding 12 rounds every week.

During these exertions, it is still important to keep the spine straight, and not bent in either directions, as muscle spasms in the neck or back may occur, due to the rapid abdominal movements.

To begin, you should start with a slow cycle of 10 to 15 breaths per minute, and then slowly increase to 60 breaths per minute.

There are three breathing rates that you can use with *kapalabhati*:

Slow speed - one expulsion per second (60 per minute)
Medium speed - two expulsions per second (120 per minute)
Fast speed – 240 expulsions per minute [practice only under close supervision]

When a rate of 120 breaths per minute is achieved, important physiological effects take place due to the removal of carbon dioxide, and the increased oxygen concentration in the lungs - the glandular, nervous, circulatory, and digestive systems, are all stimulated. This is a very good cleansing and purifying practice for the body.

Variation 1: Kapalabhati with alternate nostril

Breathe as in the Primary technique, but instead of using both nostrils together, they are used alternately.

Apply *nasik mudra*, closing the right nostril with the right thumb. Inhale through the left nostril, allowing the abdomen to expand. Pull in the abdomen rapidly, expelling the breath from the left nostril. Close the left nostril with the ring and little finger, releasing the thumb from the right nostril. Allow inhalation to take place, as the abdomen expands. Pull in the abdomen rapidly, expelling the breath from the right nostril.

This completes one round. You should practice a minimum of 36 rounds, increasing to 144 rounds.

Bhastrika Pranayama: **Bellows Breath**

This *pranayama* is used to remove certain energetic blockages, called the three *granthis* [knots] which are along the *sushumna*, the central *nadi*. These knots or energy blocks prevent the free movement of the *prana* energy in the *sushumna*. The three knots are:

> *Brahma granthi*: located in the perineum root center
> *Vishnu granthi*: located in the navel center
> *Rudra granthi*: located in the third-eye center

When these knots are broken by the performance of *bhastrika pranayama*, the *kundalini* is free to rise gradually towards the crown center, which is the goal of *pranayama* practice, and of *Kundalini Yoga*.

The Sanskrit word *bhastrika* means 'bellows'. It's analogous to a blacksmith's bellows which blow air powerfully and rapidly in order to fan the flames of the fire. So to perform this technique, you should inhale and exhale rapidly.

The difference between *bhastrika* and *kapalabhati* is that in *bhastrika*, the inhalation is as rapid as the exhalation, whereas in *kapalabhati*, the inhalation is gentle and long, while the exhalation is rapid and forceful.

Another difference between *bhastrika* and *kapalabhati* is that in *bhastrika,* after inhalation, there is a natural breath retention, until the urge to breathe occurs, during which, there is union of the upward moving *prana* and downward moving *apana*.

Bhastrika with both nostrils

Sit comfortably in *siddhasana* or *padmasana* with the spine straight. Relax and close your eyes, keeping a smile on your face.

Inhale and exhale through both nostrils strongly and rapidly, so that the expulsions of breath follow one another in rapid succession. This will bring into rapid action both the diaphragm and the entire respiratory apparatus. One rapid inhalation and exhalation completes one *bhastrika* breath.

Practice sixteen breaths, breathing out deeply on the sixteenth expulsion, and taking a long, slow, deep inhalation through both nostrils.

Then, watch your breath, without forcing the breath retention. Due to the oxygenation of the blood with the rapid breaths, there will be a period during which you will not feel the urge to breath. Take a normal breath, when the urge arises.

This completes one round of *bhastrika*. Practice a minimum of 7 rounds. Take a short rest between each round by taking a few normal breaths. As you progress you can gradually increase the number of breaths from sixteen up to 144 in each round.

People with high blood pressure or heart problems should not practice *bhastrika*.

Variation: *Bhastrika* with Alternate Nostril

Sit in comfortably with a straight spine, and inhale deeply through both nostrils.

Apply *nasik mudra* and close your right nostril with your thumb. Exhale slowly and deeply through your left nostril. Then take a short inhalation through the left nostril and begin the *bhastrika* breathing in the left nostril for sixteen breaths.

On the sixteenth expulsion, inhale slowly and deeply through the left nostril and then watch the breath, without forcing the breath retention and slowly exhale through the left nostril.

Return to normal breathing. Take a short rest before performing the same actions with the right nostril.

Release the thumb from the right nostril, and close the left. Exhale slowly and deeply through the right nostril. Then take a short inhalation through the right nostril and begin the *bhastrika* breathing in the right nostril for sixteen breaths. On the sixteenth expulsion, inhale slowly and deeply through the right nostril and then watch the breath, without forcing the breath retention and slowly exhale through the right nostril.

This completes one round. You should start with 3 rounds, increasing gradually to sixteen rounds.

Section C
Life Force Expansion Pranayama

Expansion Pranayama Series

When there is an expansion of life-force, there is, in addition to the increase in health, an expansion of consciousness, leading to higher meditative states.

Ujjayi Pranayama

This is the "victorious breath" and is also commonly called the psychic breath. Its practice makes us attentive and gradually more aware, expanding our life-force and consequently, our consciousness.

> *Closing the mouth, draw the breath up*
> *with an audible sound through both nostrils,*
> *till the breath fills the space between the throat and the heart.*
> *Do kumbhaka as before, and exhale through the left nostril.*
> *This removes phlegm from the throat and*
> *stimulates digestive fire. It is called ujjayi,*
> *and can be done while, moving, standing, sitting or walking.*
> Hatha Yoga Pradipika 2:51,52,53

Ujjayi Pranayama can be practiced safely without breath retention, at any time and in all positions, such as during postures practice, standing and walking. To balance the *prana* and *apana*, use both nostrils to keep the length of the inhalation and exhalation the same.

Ujjayi calms the mind and nervous system and relieves hypertension, anxiety and depression, slowing the heartbeat and reducing high blood pressure. It is therefore very helpful for people suffering from insomnia, asthma, pulmonary diseases and heart diseases. When awareness follows the breath, it develops concentration, and moves one to a meditative state.

Basic Ujjayi

Sit in a comfortable meditative posture, close your eyes and relax.

With your mouth closed, become aware of the breath in the nostrils, as the air moves in and out, in a calm and rhythmic manner. Practice *sukha pranayama* for a minute or so.

Then, move your awareness to the throat, feeling the breath moving in and out through the throat.

As the breathing becomes deeper, and smoother, gently contract the glottis, closing it partially. This will cause a "snoring" sound to be made with the inhalation, and a hissing sound to be made during the exhalation.

As you get the hang of the "ujjayi" sound, in the throat, incorporate the Full Yogic Breath, from Part 1, with the concentration still centered in the throat. The sound should not cause the straining of the muscles, but should still be audible to someone close by.

Perform sixteen rounds, gradually increasing to forty-eight rounds.

Variation: Ujjayi with *kevala*

First perform sixteen rounds of normal *ujjayi*. Then after inhaling with both nostrils on the seventeenth round, completely close the glottis and watch the breath without forced retention.

When the urge to breathe arises, exhale slowly with *ujjayi*. Then watch the breath, until the urge to breathe arises, and then inhale with *ujjayi*, and so on for another fifteen rounds.

The following two practices are normally called cooling *pranayama*, because they can be used to cool down the body when it is overheating. However, there is also a deeper significance that may be missed, and oral tradition suggests that they are useful in expanding our awareness, by letting us feel parts of our anatomy that we normally do not pay much attention to.

Sitkari Pranayama

Putting the tongue between the lips,
inhale through the mouth with a hissing sound,
and then exhale through the two nostrils.
This is called sitkari and its practice
will enhance your beauty.
Hath Yoga Pradipika 2:54

Sitkari means "hissing", and describes the sound that is made when performing this *pranayama*.

Sit in one of the recommended postures, with your spine straight. Close your eyes and hold the teeth tightly together, while separating the lips, and exposing the teeth. Fold the tip of the tongue inwards and press it to the upper palate. The folded tongue should come slightly out between the upper and lower rows of teeth, so that there will two narrow openings on both sides.

Inhale slowly through the two sides with a hissing sound. Be sensitive to the areas that the breath goes over. Then close your mouth, and exhale the warm air through the two nostrils, feeling its effect on the surfaces that it passes. This completes one round. Perform sixteen rounds.

Traditionally, *sitkari* is said to enable the sincere practitioner to master all desires.

Sitkari Pranayama

Figure 27. Sitkari Pranayama

Sitali Pranayama

> *The intelligent practitioner will suck the air*
> *through the (beak of the) tongue,*
> *perform kumbhaka as before,*
> *and exhale through the two nostrils.*
> *This kumbhaka is called sitali*
> *and cures enlarged stomach or spleen,*
> *and other conditions ill-health,*
> *such as fever, hunger and thirst.*
> Hatha Yoga Pradipika 2:57,58

Sitali is a cooling *pranayama*, and has a cooling and soothing effect on the body, and can be practiced sitting in a meditative asana or standing.

This *pranayama* cools the system and induces relaxation to the body and tranquility to the mind. It purifies the blood, improves digestion and quenches thirst. The area over which the cooling air moves over is different than that of *sitkari*, and the two awaken different levels of awareness.

On a deeper level, *sitali* soothes and helps to overcome the passions.

Sit in one of the recommended postures. Place hands in *chin mudra*.

Stick your tongue out just past the lips and curl or fold it lengthwise to form a tube, or the beak. Inhale slowly and deeply through this tube, with a hissing sound, until your lungs are filled completely. Withdraw your tongue, close your mouth, and slowly exhale through both nostrils.

This technique can be practiced daily beginning with sixteen rounds and gradually increasing to forty-eight rounds.

It is best practiced after asana and other strenuous *pranayama* practice.

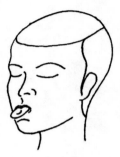

Sitali Pranayama

Figure 28. Sitali Pranayama

Section D
Life Force Transformation
Pranayama

Laya Pranayama Techniques

Laya means to 'dissolve', and what is dissolved is the normal consciousness. These techniques are not usually given the importance that are their due, because of the lack of explanation of how they fit into the overall scheme of *pranayama*. *bhramari* and *murchha pranayamas* function to dissolve normal awareness, and lead to deeper levels of experience.

Bhramari Pranayama: **Humming Bee Breath**

Inhale normally with the air producing a humming sound like that of a male bee, and exhale much slower than the inhalation, making the humming sound of a female bee. Yogis perform this pranayama for long durations to get an ecstatic state of mind.
Hatha Yoga Pradipika 2:68

Sit in one of the recommended *padmasana*, or *vajrasana*, close your eyes and relax, especially the jaws.

Inhale deeply through both nostrils while making a high pitched humming sound. Exhale slowly though your nostrils, with your mouth closed, making a lower-pitched sound, like the humming of a female bee, and feeling the vibration in the head.

Do this three times, and then raise the arms sideways, bending the elbows, and close off your ears with your index fingers. Breathe normally, listening for any internal sounds and focusing on the third-eye to see the internal light. Do this for one to three minutes. This completes one round.

Perform three rounds, gradually increasing to seven rounds.

After a little practice, *bhramari* will improve the quality of your voice, making it sweet and melodious. It is also good for throat ailments, calms the mind and reduces blood pressure. During deep practice, it will awaken *nada*, the inner sound.

With further practice, certain internal sounds will be heard [refer Gheranda Samhita], with the unfolding of the awareness of each succeeding energy center. Even *samadhi* or the state of bliss, caused by the dissolving of the seer, seeing and seen, is possible with *bhramari pranayama*.

Figure 29. Bhramari Pranayama

Murcha Pranayama

*Perform kumbhaka with comfort and then
withdraw the attention from external objects
and focus on the third-eye between the eyebrows.
This causes a swooning of the mind,
and leads to happiness.*
Gheranda Samhita 5:83

Murcha means 'to swoon' but also 'to expand'. This *pranayama* will expand consciousness and induce inner awareness with relaxation.

Those who suffer from heart disease, high blood pressure or vertigo, should avoid the practice of *murcha*.

Sit in *vajrasana, siddhasana, padmasana* with your hands on your knees, so that you are seated firmly and steady.

Perform sixteen rounds of *bhastrika pranayama*, to oxygenate the blood, and then inhale slowly and deeply, taking a complete *Yogic* Breath. While watching the breath, lower the chin to the hollow of the neck, and keeping your arms straight, pressing your knees with your hands. When the urge to breath arises, raise your head and exhale slowly through the nostrils, relaxing the arms at the same time. Relax and experience the calmness and tranquility, for a few minutes, and then repeat two more times, for a total of three rounds.

Then, with your eyes open, gaze upward at the spiritual eye, the point between the eyebrows, *shambhavi mudra* [refer figure 31.] With the eyes held steadily, hold for as long as possible. Internalize your one-pointed awareness at the spiritual eye. Let the mind and breath become absorbed in contemplation.

After a few minutes, take a complete *Yogic* breath, and then bend your head backwards keeping your eyes open, and maintaining the concentrating at the point between the eyebrows.

Watch the breath until the urge to exhale arises, keeping your arms straight, pressing your knees with your hands. Exhale slowly as you relax your arms and close your eyes, bringing your head back to the upright position.

Relax and experience the calmness and tranquility for a few minutes. Repeat two more times for a total of three rounds.

Figure 30. Murcha Pranayama

Rudra Shivananda

Advice on setting up a *Pranayama* practice

It is best to have access to a qualified teacher with experience in *pranayama*. Many techniques have been introduced in the previous sections, and many more techniques and variations are taught in different schools of *Hatha Yoga*.

The ones covered here are considered the major ones and form the core practice of all the lineages. Beginners become very confused by the plethora of techniques and wonder how to get started, and form a stable and consistent practice.

The following is a suggested schedule based on the experience of generations of practitioners:

- The complete 'Yogic Breath ', which was introduced in Part 1, should be practiced for at least twice a day for one month, so that it becomes comfortable and automatic, when you sit for *pranayama*.

- Learn the 'Yogic Energization' techniques, and then add the preliminary cleansing and warming-up exercises

- The primary practice consists of the 6 parts of the *anuloma-viloma pranayama* set. These should be practiced for at least one year. You can try out the different variations, and then choose the ones that you feel best about, and they will form the your main series. If on any day, you are rushed for time, and can only perform one of them, always do *nadi shuddhi*.

- Learn the purification *pranayamas*. Even though this is learned after the *anuloma-viloma* series, they should be practiced after the cleansing and warm-up, and before the main series.

- After about one year of *pranayama* practice, you may add the Expansion series, such as *ujjayi*, and the cooling techniques. These are done after the main series.

- After 2 years of *pranayama* practice, the *Laya* series are added. They are always done at the end, usually after the Expansion series.

- A complete practice, would consist of at least one of each of the cleansing, purification, *anuloma-viloma*, expansion, and *laya* sets.

- A consistent daily practice is the key to success.

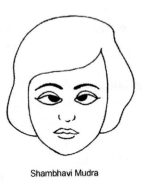

Shambhavi Mudra

Figure 31. Shambavi Mudra

Part 3
Applications of the
Science of Breath
Swara Yoga and Pranic Healing

The discipline and practice of *pranayama* is primarily for the awakening of the spiritual potential in the body-mind complex. However, due to the expansion and absorption of life-force energy, there is a concurrent increase in the health of the body-mind complex, with self-healing of physical, emotional and mental problems. These more visible healing effects are indirect by-products of the deeper spiritual healing being brought about by the expansion of consciousness.

In this section, we are going to learn some of the direct applications of the yogic science of breath to direct healing, and to various human activities.

Pranic healing is part of the ancient science of *Ayurveda*, the holistic science of health and well-being. According to *Ayurveda*, all diseases are caused by *pranic* imbalance, which can range from blocked prana, to low *prana*, to excessive *prana*. The methods of healing, whether through herbs, diets, oils, bodywork with healing hands, gemstones, mantras, or breath-work, are all ways to re-distribute *prana*.

The *Nath yogis*, have also given us the science of *Swara Yoga*, a manifold application of the observation, that normally, we are breathing, with one of our nostrils dominant, that is breath flows freely through it, while the other nostril is more or less blocked. This nostril dominance has an approximately one and half hour alternating cycle, such that if the left nostril is currently dominant, then, in the next cycle, the right nostril will assume dominance.

This curious fact, by itself, would not be of much use, if not, for the linkage between the breath and the mind. In this particular case, it was found that when the breath flowed through the left nostril, the mind was more inwardly active, with an increase in artistic and intuitive powers.

When the breath flowed through the right nostril, the mind was more outwardly active, focused on external events, with an increase in analytical powers. These mental states correspond to the dominance of the two parts of the human brain – the right brain for intuition, and the left brain for rational thought. Yogis have long known about this correlation, and used it to harmonize the breath, and the concomitant mental state, with essential life activities.

Swara Yoga

Swara and Health

According to the science of *Swara*, for optimum health, one should maximize the flow of *ida* during the day and the flow of *pingala* during the night. This translates to breathing more from the left nostril to cool the body and counteract the heating effects of daytime. On the other hand, to offset the cooling effect of the night, you should breath more from the right nostril, by sleeping on your left side.

However, excessive dominance of one nostril over a long period of time, generally is a signal of ill-health. Excessive flow of *ida nadi* has been found to be an indicator of digestive problems [insufficient fire for the digestive process], as well as problems with the respiratory and sexual reproductive systems. The excessive flow of *pingala nadi*, may be indicative of ulcers and hypertension.

Before a disorder has set in, it may be possible to prevent its onslaught, by changing the dominance of the nostril. However, once the symptoms have strongly manifested, then changing the dominance cannot reverse the disease, but may bring some relief from the symptoms. For example, if one feels a headache coming on, you can check for the dominant nostril, close it and start breathing from the other nostril for about 15 minutes.

The Sanskrit word *swara* is from the root *swar*, 'to sound'. *Swara Yoga* is the ancient science of studying the flow of the life-force, *prana*, and is also known as *Swarodaya*.

The science of Swarodaya (knowledge of the rise of
breathing in one or the other nostril) is higher
than the highest of the holy scriptures
and is like the lamp's wick, like the spirit
which illuminates the body.
Shivaswarodaya 27

The *yogis* of India studying this science experimented and compiled detailed correlations between the way the breath flowed and various physiological and psychological states. They measured the various distances from the nose that the exhalation of air can be felt during a person's different activities [refer the Gheranda Samhita]. Unfortunately, no recent scientific work has been done to verify their monumental undertaking. Some examples are given:

Normal state	4 ½ inches
Agitated	9 inches
Singing	12 inches
Eating	15 inches
Walking	18 inches
Sleeping	22 inches
Sexual intercourse	27 inches
Physical exercise	more than 27 inches

You can measure your own breath by moistening the back of your hand and holding it under your nostrils. Move your hand forward and backward from the nose. As you exhale you will feel the air blowing on to your skin. Measure the length of your breath from nose to hand.

Swara Yoga on Death and Longevity

If the breath of a person flows through one nostril t
hroughout the night, then his life
will end within three years.
Shivaswarodaya 331

Put your hand on your forehead
And look,
If you see the breath rhythm unchanged
Well and good;
If you see it enlarged,
Death awaits in six months
If you see it doubled,
In a month shalt life depart.
Tirumandirum 770

Both *Tirumoolar* and the scribe of the *Shivaswarodaya* give many examples of forecasting the end of physical life. **These statements should be taken with extreme caution, because only very experienced practitioners of *pranayama* have the sensitivity and knowledge to utilize the information from their breathing patterns to forecast something like illness and death.**

Even modern physicians understand that a person who breathes shallowly in short, sharp gasps is likely to reduce his or her life-span, compared with a person who breathes slowly and deeply. The ancient *yogis* actually measured a person's life-span, not in years but by the number of breaths. They considered that each individual is allocated a fixed number of breaths in their lifetime, with the number varying from person to person. Therefore if a person breathes slowly and deeply, they not only gain more vitality but they also maximize their life-span.

These *yogis* lived in the forests of India, or in secluded mountains, and so were able to study wild animals in their natural environment. They discovered that animals with a slow breathing rate, such as elephants and tortoises, have a long life-span. Conversely, they noticed that animals with a fast breathing rate, such as birds and rabbits, live only for a few years. These observations probably helped them realize the importance of slow breathing. It is said by the *yogis* that a normal person breathes 21,600 breaths a day and lives a shorter life than some of animals that breathe less.

They were also able to directly relate respiration to the heartbeat. Slow respiration occurs with a slow beating heart, which means the heart has to work less, which corresponds to a longer life. For example, an elephant's heart beats at approximately 25 times per minute, while a mouse's heart, on the other hand beat's approximately 1,000 times a minute.

These *yogis* put their research into practice, and were able to live very long lives, through the practice of *pranayama* and meditation. They even achieved mastery and control over the life-force of the body, attaining the power to shed the physical body at will or to retain it for an indefinite period of time.

Yogananda stated in his spiritual classic, "Autobiography of a Yogi" that *Lahiri Mahasaya* had a very famous friend called *Swami Trailanga*, who was reputed to be over 300 years old. He also introduced to the world, the great-grandmaster of *Kriya Yoga*, *Babaji*. The immortal *Babaji* has developed control over time, decay and death, and can materialize or de-materialize his physical body at will. His immortal body requires no food and he appears to his spiritually advanced disciples in the Himalayas from time to time. He has appeared to his advanced disciples, even in very recent times.

By the application of *Swara Yoga, asanas, pranayama*, deep meditation and selfless devotion for God and mankind, we can prevent disease, preserve health and youth, and promote longevity.

Swara Yoga and baby gender

> *On the fifth day after menses, perform intercourse*
> *to give birth to a male child, when the man's right nostril is*
> *open, while the woman's left nostril is dominant.*
> Shivaswarodaya 286

The ancient scientists of breath were practical in satisfying the demands of the people of their time. The general population seems to have the same needs then as now. Some couples would like to pre-determine the gender of their child. The general rule is for a couple who wants a female child, to have intercourse on the fifteenth day after the woman's menstruation has stopped, and to make sure that the man's left nostril is dominant, while the woman's right nostril is dominant.

On the other hand, for those who desire a male child, intercourse should be on the fifth day after menstruation stops; the man's right nostril should be dominant, while the woman's left should be dominant. Refer to the section on '*Swara Yoga* for Intentional *Pranic* Control', for ways to change the nostril dominance.

They were also concerned about the health and beauty of their child. The following gives the consequences of conceiving a female baby on various days after completion of menstruation:

Fifth	physical problems
Seventh	old age problems
Ninth	indolence
Eleventh	loose morals
Thirteenth	bad marriage
Fifteenth	achieve highest potential

Swara Yoga and prana (flow of life-force)

The scientists of *prana* found that during the course of a day, the flow of air or *prana* is flowing more in either the *ida nadi* (left nostril) or the *pingala nadi* (right nostril), or evenly flowing through the *sushumna nadi* (both nostrils). You can test this for yourself by moistening the back of the hand and breathing on it, to feel in which nostril the air is flowing more predominantly, or block one of the nostrils at a time and breathing through the other. You will find that the flow of air through the nostrils is very rarely equal.

Under normal circumstances, when the breath and the *nadis* are functioning normally, the breath flow alternates between the left and the right nostril. Modern scientists have confirmed this phenomenon, but have not discovered either the cause or purpose of this alternating breath flow, aside from speculating that it may help to regulate the body's temperature. *Swara yogis* have through their insight, claimed that the alternation of the natural breath flow in each nostril is due to biological changes caused by the mind's fluctuating mental states, as well as to environmental and lunar influences.

A few of the observations from the scientists of *Swara* concerning this phenomena, in relation to the moon, are given, just to demonstrate the depth and thoroughness of these yogic scientists:

- The *ida nadi* is dominant at sunrise, on the first lunar day when the moon is waxing.

- The breath flow alternates between *ida* and *pingala*, at the end of each hour.

- The breath flow continues alternating every hour for three days.

- On the fourth day at sunrise the *pingala nadi* becomes dominant.

- On the first lunar day, when the moon is waning, there is breath reversal at sunrise, and *pingala nadi* becomes dominant.

Right now, you might be wondering why the *yogis* spent so much time observing the flow of breath. **It's because they found the significant fact that a person's mental state would change with the change in nostril dominance.** When the breath flow is dominant in the right nostril a person is more inclined to physical action than to thinking or intellectual pursuits. This is because the right nostril is associated with the solar current, warmth, heat, action and the physical. It is also associated with left brain activities, such as analytic, logical and linear thinking.

When the left nostril is dominant, the mental state becomes peaceful, calm, almost dreamy. The cool moon current influences the right brain tendencies of introspection, mental creativity and higher intuition.

It has also been found that this natural rhythm changes with our fluctuating mental and emotional states, activities, disease, stress and the unbalancing of our daily routines. This natural rhythmic cycle is necessary for balancing the mind and body. There would be an imbalance, and serious harm can occur, if the breath were to flow in only one nostril for 24 hours or more, an indication of serious illness.

When the breath is flowing equally through both nostrils, then the *sushumna* nadi is active and successful meditation is possible. In this balanced state, the mental processes become clear and calm while the body and the breath becomes steady and calm. If the *pingala* is flowing, the body will be restless and when the *ida* flows, there will be distracting thoughts.

Swara Yoga for intentional *pranic* control

The *prana* scientists, did not just observe the changing flow of breath, with its consequent dramatic effects, they also developed techniques for intentionally changing the flow, to suit one's needs.

They have given various methods for changing the flow of breath in the *nadis*. If you wish to change the flow from the right nostril to the left, you can use any of the following methods. The reverse process can be used to change from left to right.

- Lie down on your right side for ten minutes. *Yogis* usually sleep on their right side with the *ida* or left nostril flow open for a calm, relaxing sleep. If the *pingala* flows predominantly at night you may become restless and find it difficult to sleep.

- Squeeze your left hand under your right arm, so that the fingers are pressing into the right armpit.

- Close off your right nostril with a piece of cotton wool for a few minutes, until the flow changes to the left nostril.

When the body is steady in asana and the spine straight, the mind becomes quiet and concentrated, letting the *sushumna* become active. To balance the *nadis* by changing the flow to the *sushumna*, concentrate at the third-eye between the eyebrows.

Swara Yoga and the Five Cosmic Elements

The ancient Masters of Wisdom perceived reality directly, and have transmitted their insights on cosmic evolution through countless generations. They perceived that cosmic consciousness gave rise to Universal Energy which then manifested into the five Universal Elements –Material Building Blocks of Space, Air, Fire, Water and Earth - which became the atomic building blocks of all matter and energy, through a process of grossification.

It is important to keep in mind that the translation of the these words is imperfect and should not lead you to confuse them with their common usage. When the Masters talk about Space, they are more closely pointing out the universal force of gravitation than anything resembling "open space".

From Universal Energy, the vibration of OM caused the appearance of Space [*Akasha*], which moved and created AIR [*Vayu*], and from the function of it's movement, SPACE created the Fire [*Agni*] element. From the heat of Fire, Space dissolved and liquefied and gave birth to Water [*Apas*]. When the Water element solidified, Earth [*Prithvi*] is formed. The whole of the material Universe is formed by the combinations of these five Elements.

It should be noted that these five Elements are not visible particles, but through a process of grossification, became present in all matter and energy. They refer to the etheric, gaseous, radiant, fluid, and solid states of matter and the principles of space movement, light, cohesion, and density.

As an example, the planet Earth is formed with a greater proportion of the gross aspects of the Earth Element.

The five bodies of man are formed by various proportions of these five Elements. In the physical body, the solid structures such as bones, muscles, skin and hair are derived from the Earth Element. From Water Element, all the fluids and secretions are derived, while the Fire Element rules the digestive and metabolic systems. All movement of the body is governed by Air, while cavities are the province of Space.

The five Elements also manifest in the five senses, providing for all perception of external environment. Space, Air, Fire, Water, and Earth are related to hearing, touch, vision, taste and smell respectively. Since the human body (all five bodies) are a manifestation of the five Elements, a balance of harmony of these are required for healing and health, as well as for spiritual realization.

The path to Self-realization must start through an understanding and passage through the Primary Elements.

Swara Yoga has given us techniques to observe the presence of the five Elements in one's physical body. It is taught that our feelings and emotions are conditioned by the particular Element which is dominating at a particular time.

Therefore, by identifying the dominant Element, and observing its progression, one can gain insight into one's consciousness. By understanding this play of the Elements, the play of consciousness is penetrated, and by passing beyond the Elements, Self-Realization is achieved.

According to *Shiva Swarodaya* v.71, the Air Element flows first, followed by Fire, Earth, Water, and Space. During a one hour period, each Element dominates for a specific time:

> Earth : 20 minutes
> Water : 16 minutes
> Fire : 12 minutes
> Air : 8 minutes
> Space : 4 minutes

My favorite technique for detecting which of the five Elements is active, at a particular time in the body, is to sense the location of air passing through the nostril. This takes some sensitivity and training, but is worth the effort. There is also some differences as to the correspondence between the location and the Element.

Some texts state that when air passes through the center of the nostril, then the Earth Element is dominant, upper part is for the Fire Element, lower part for the Water Element; while when air passes obliquely, it is the Air Element, and when it is rotating, then the Space Element is present.

My own experience is that when air passes the top of the nostril, it corresponds to the Earth Element; bottom to Water; right side to Fire; left side to Air; center to Space.

More research needs to be done on this aspect of the science of Swara.

Applying Breath in asana practice

When breath is integrated with the practice of the yoga postures, a deeper level is experienced. The practice of postures, guided by the life-force, and with awareness, is transformed into meditation. With breath and awareness, the postures are no longer just physical exercises.

In asana practice, there are general rules for integrating your breath:

- Breath awareness is constant, even when your body is stationary.

- There should be no forced holding of breath during any of the phases of an asana, whether static or dynamic.

- Inhalation occurs as you extend the spine, exhalation when you release tension and relax.

- Inhale when you move to the center or become erect and exhale when moving away from a centered position.

- Inhale into a pose and exhale to release the pose.

- Use *ujjayi* breathing to harmonize your body and mind.

- Rhythmic breathing, especially equal length breathing is used to harmonize the body motions.

- Breath can be used to release specific tension areas that restrict the breath or body sensations.

To illustrate some of these principles, we can use the simple example of a standing posture where you lift and lower your hands. When you lift the arms up, inhale during this motion, and learn to pace the tempo with the time required to fill your lungs. In this manner, the inhalation will be complete when the arms reach a vertical position reaching for the ceiling. Then, exhale to lower your arms to the sides, such that all the lungs are emptied, when the arms reach the final position.

Do this a number of times, and keep awareness of both the motion and the breath.

Next, inhale and bring the hands together at the heart level. Stretch your arms to the side with the exhalation. Repeat a number of times to synchronize your breathing with the motion. Exhale and relax your arms back along the sides of your body.

In a third exercise, inhale in the centered position, and then slowly twist to the left with an exhalation. Return to the center with an inhalation, and then twist to the right with the exhalation. Do this a number of times, keeping awareness of both the motion and the breath.

Finally, bend forward about 12 inches with an exhalation and return to a centered erect posture on an inhalation. Perform this action with awareness for about six times.

The co-ordination of movement with breath as shown in the above examples will become second nature to all your physical movements, with practice and constant awareness.

.

Health by Pranic Healing

Although the *pranayama* techniques presented in Part 2, have therapeutic benefits, they are generally practiced more for their spiritual benefits. There are some *pranayamas* that are primarily therapeutic in nature, and are practiced for their health benefits.

From our experience, it would be reasonable to conclude that all methods of healing that do not resort to physical paraphernalia, such as drugs or herbs, are really direct or indirect ways of awakening *prana* within a "dis-eased" body. Unnatural living and improper breathing can unbalance the *pranic* currents within the body and give rise to various disorders and diseases.

By practicing *pranayama* correctly and regularly, you will have access to a store of *prana*, which you will be able to use for self-healing or for healing others. The key to successful *pranic* healing is will-power and concentration to direct the flow of *prana* to any part of the body, whether it is your own or someone else's.

Ayurveda and pranic healing

According to the ancient health science of India, called *Ayurveda*, all forms of matter are made up of the combination and condensation of the five Cosmic Elements [introduced in a previous section], of Space, Air, Fire, Water, and Earth. Although all material things are constituted from all Five Elements, they are differentiated according to the proportion of each Element.

This knowledge is applied to the human body and constitution, through the system of classification, called the *doshas*. In matter where the Air Element predominates, it is described as having a *vata* constitution or *dosha*. There are three primary *doshas* used to describe the human body. Besides *vata dosha*, when Fire predominates, it is called *pitta*, and *kapha* for the predominance of Water.

Every human body may be classified into one of the three *doshas*. There are a small number of people, who may be combinations of more than one *dosha*, for example *pitta-kapha*, or *vata-pitta*.

On one level, our physical body has all three *doshas* working together. For example, the digestive system is *pitta* or Fiery in nature, the nervous system is *vata* or Airy, while tissues are *kapha* or Watery. This perspective helps in understanding how *yoga* practice, particularly *pranayama* affects the various organs and systems of the body.

At a higher level, one of the *doshas* predominates, not only the body structure, but also tendencies towards specific types of ill-health, as well as emotional reactions. This perspective helps to understand the affects of yoga practice on the three distinct body-emotion-mind types. Different foods are prescribed for the three *doshas*, and each has a set of 'beneficial' and 'harmful' table of foods, for attaining optimal health. Similarly, it is necessary to adapt yoga practice according to the body type. For example, *pitta* types should perform more 'cooling' *pranayamas*, and less 'heating' *pranayamas*.

There are certain generalizations which are helpful to prevent ill-health: *vata* types are prone to mental or nervous disorders, *pitta* types have a tendency towards inflammations and infections, while *kapha* types suffer from overweight and swollen glands.

All doshic imbalances can be alleviated by proper diet, and in most cases, a balancing of the five *vayus* or *pranas*, which have been explained in Part 2.

The two most important *vayus* are *prana* and *apana*, and they can be balanced by the alternate nostril breathing techniques. For those who are lethargic, *ujayii pranayama* is stimulating, sending *prana* to the head, throat and heart.

The following set of healing *pranayama* balances all five *pranas*, and is highly recommended as a disease preventive, as well as helping in the treatment of diseases. It consists of six *pranic* techniques, which I've personally found very beneficial, and would like to share with you. Each has a different function, and effect different parts of the *pranic* or Energy Body:

- *vayu* balancing: balances the five *pranas*
- toxin removal: surface treatment
- polarity balancing: central channel
- storage and distribution: throughout the body
- *prana mudra*: for the *chakras*
- *pranic* self-Healing: front, back, left & right channels

Vayu Balancing Pranayama

Since there are five *pranas*, or five aspects of the life-force energy in the body, there are five parts to the balancing technique. During the practice, each part is repeated a number of times, and then proceeding to the next part, in the sequence. Finally, the sequence is reversed and each part is practiced for the same number of repetitions.

The *pranayama* is given as a sequence incorporating all the techniques, but each can be performed by itself, if you feel the need to balance a particular *vayu*, or aspect of *prana*.

1. *Prana Vayu*

Inhale deeply, drawing energy from above and around the head, into the third-eye center, visualizing a ball of light concentrated there.

Exhale through the third eye, spreading the life-force throughout the head, and the eyes, ears, nostrils, and the mouth.

Life-force is brought in all around the head through the senses, purifying them.

Repeat seven times.

Benefits:
Revitalizes the brain and helps against disorders of the nervous system. It is useful as treatment for sinus problems, head colds, and headaches.

2. *Udana Vayu*

Inhale deeply through the mouth and draw the life-force into the throat center.

Exhale, chanting OM aloud, feeling the vibration expanding outward and upward.

Repeat seven times.

Benefits:
Increases vitality and improves self-expression.
Helpful in treatment of sore throat.

3. *Vyana Vayu*

Inhale deeply through the heart center, while extending your arms to the sides and opening up the chest. The life-force energy is spiraling outwards. At the end of the inhalation, visualize the life-force expanding throughout the body and limbs.

Exhale back into the heart center, visualizing all the life-force returning to the heart center, spiraling inwards.

Repeat seven times.

Benefits:
Helpful in treating diseases of circulatory problems, especially lung and heart diseases.

4. *Samana Vayu*

Feel the navel center, and visualize the universal life-force through its galaxies, stars and planets.

Inhale deeply, bringing the universal life-force into the navel center, spiraling inwards.

Feel the life-force as concentrated fire at the navel at the end of the inhalation.

Exhale, spiraling outward nourishing all the cells, organs and systems of the body.

Repeat seven times.

Benefits:
Helpful in treating digestive system disorders and diseases of the liver and gall-bladder.

5. *Apana Vayu*

This is best done in a standing posture. Feel the perineum and visualize the connection with the center of the earth.

Inhale deeply, drawing the life-force energy down to the root center at the perineum.

Exhale from the perineum, down through the legs and feet, into the earth.

Repeat seven times.

Benefits:

Helpful in treating disorders of the reproduction and the excretory systems. Also useful for healing menstrual problems and sexual dysfunctions.

After practicing the sequence from steps 1 to 5, then reverse and practice from 5 to 1.

Toxin Removal Pranayama

The breath is packed under pressure within the blood, and forced to release the carbon dioxide waste through the millions of pores in the skin. When the carbon dioxide is discharged, it increases the temperature of the skin, causing perspiration and the discharging of toxins.

This *pranayama* also purifies the skin and makes the skin softer and healthier. It is good for such skin conditions as acne, psoriasis, and eczema.

This practice should be done in a well-ventilated room, with the floor covered with a thick rug or cushions.

Procedure:
- Sit in *vajrasana* with the eyes closed and a smile on your face
- Inhale slowly and deeply through both nostrils.
- Retain the breath for a moment
- Inhale some more, and hold for another moment
- For a third time, inhale if you still can
- Exhale very slowly through both nostrils.
- Practice two more rounds
- Lie down and relax totally

Polarity Balancing or Sun/Moon Pranayama

Each body cell has a polarity, magnetic in quality like the earth. When these cells are aligned and brought into balance then the energy body and physical body become balanced. The alignment of the cells is accomplished by drawing positive solar and negative lunar currents of *pranic* energy through the body.

This technique should be done in a well-ventilated room, with the floor covered by a thick rug or cushions.

- Lie on the floor in a relaxation pose with your head pointing north and your feet pointing south. Close your eyes and relax.
- Practice twelve round of *sukha Pranayama* without breath retention. The ratio is 12:0:12:0, that is inhalation for 12 counts, no retention with breath in, exhalation for 12 counts, and no retention with breath out.
- Now visualize the warmth and energy of the sun just over your head. Inhale this solar energy through the top of your head, gradually drawing it down to your feet, visualizing a warm golden *prana* flowing with the inhaling breath through your body. Allow the energy to stream out through the soles of your feet.
- Retain the breath for just a moment, and visualize and feel a cool lunar energy below your feet. Exhale from the feet up to the head, visualizing a cool silvery *prana* flowing through your body.
- Practice 12 rounds slowly and rhythmically. Then rest in deep relaxation.

Prana Storage and Distribution

In order to preserve the body in good health, *Mahasiddha Tirumoolar* also counseled that the *prana* should be held in the body.

> *If the body perishes, prana departs*
> *Nor will the light of Truth be reached*
> *I learned the way of the preserving the body*
> *And so doing, my prana too.*
> **Tirumandirum 724**

The life-force energy is brought into and initially stored in the navel center. From this *manipura chakra*, the life-force can be distributed to all parts of the body for self-Healing.

- Lie down on your back with the eyes closed, and completely relax.
- Place your left hand lightly just above the navel, and your right hand over the left.
- Breathe slowly and rhythmically.
- With each inhalation mentally direct the *prana*, in the form of blue light to the solar plexus.
- With each exhalation direct and visualize this healing *prana* spreading throughout every part of the body.
- Distribute it to every bone, muscle, organ, nerve and cell.
- Concentrate at the point between your eyebrows and feel the *prana* being stored in your body.
- Repeat this three times.

Prana Mudra

A tonic to awaken and distribute *prana shakti* healing energy throughout the body, for releasing physical, emotional and mental blockages. It establishes equanimity and connectedness to the universal source of all energy. This technique is best practiced at sunrise, preferably, facing the sun.

1. Sit in one of the recommended postures, preferably *siddhasana*. Place the right palm on top of the left palm. Close the eyes and relax the whole body, yet maintaining a straight back.

Figure 32. Prana Mudra position 1

2. Utilizing the abdominal breathing, inhale and exhale deeply, expelling the maximum amount of air from the lungs, by contracting the abdominal muscles. While the breath is held out for a moment, contract the perineum and the anal sphincter.

Figure 33. Prana Mudra position 2

3. While maintaining the contraction of the *mulabandha*, begin inhaling slowly, expanding the abdomen fully to draw in the maximum air into the lungs. At the same time, raise the hands to the level of the navel center. The hands are not touching, with fingers pointing towards each other and the palms facing inwards. There should be no tension in the

arms. During the inhalation, feel and visualize the *prana* or life-force being drawn from the *muladhara chakra* to the *manipura chakra* along the spinal column.

4. Continue with thoracic breathing, expanding the chest and simultaneously raising the hands to the heart center. Feel the *prana* rising from the navel to the heart along the spine.

Figure 34. Prana Mudra position 3

5. Complete the inhalation with clavicular breathing, raising the shoulders slightly and drawing some more air into the lungs. Feel the life-force energy being drawn from the heart

center to the throat center, as you raise your hands to the front of the throat.

Figure 35. Prana Mudra position 4

6. Retain the breath for a moment, as you spread the arms to the sides, palm facing upwards and out-stretched near ear level. Feel the life force rising from the throat up the head to the crown, and spreading out from the top of the head and emanating all around you. Release the *mulabhanda*.

Figure 36. Prana Mudra position 5

7. Begin exhalation, by lowering the shoulders and returning the hands to its position in front of the throat, feeling the *prana* descending to the *vishuddhi chakra*. Contract the chest muscles, and lowering the hands to the heart center, as the *prana* descends to the *anahata chakra*. Complete the exhalation by contracting the abdomen, lowering the hands to the navel, as the *prana* descends to the *manipura chakra*. At the end of the exhalation, the hands are resting on top of the thighs, as at the beginning of the cycle.

8. Repeat twice more and then completely relax.

self-Healing Pranayama

- Lie down on the floor with your eyes closed in a relaxation pose.
- Visualize a radiant ball of white light just above the crown of your head.
- Inhale to a count of twelve seconds through both nostrils, while visualizing and feeling that you are drawing in a stream of pure white healing *prana* through the soles of your feet up to your head, energizing and rejuvenating your whole body.
- Exhale to a count of twelve seconds, visualizing a steam of pure white *prana* flowing down from your head to your feet and out through the soles, cleansing all the toxins from your body.
- Repeat 5 times, for a total of six rounds.
- Begin long, slow, deep rhythmic breaths for a few minutes.
- Inhale and visualize healing *pranic* energy flowing from the soles of your feet up the back of your body to your head.
- Exhale from your face down the front of your body to your feet.
- Circulate the *prana* from back to front six times.
- Now, visualize the *prana* flowing up the front of your body with the inhalation and flowing down the back with the exhalation. Do this six times.
- Inhale and visualize the *prana* flowing from left to right six times.
- Inhale and visualize the *pranic* energy flowing from right to left six times.
- Relax completely and concentrate on the spiritual eye for a few minutes.

Rudra Shivananda

Appendix

Bandhas

When electricity is generated, it is necessary to have transformers, conductors, fuses, switches and so forth, to carry the power to its destination, otherwise it would be useless or harmful. So also, when *prana* is made to flow in the yogi's body, it is necessary for him to employ *bandhas*, to prevent the dissipation of energy and to transport it to the right places. They are also practiced to awaken the *kundalini* and direct its energy up the central channel, called *sushumna nadi*.

Bandha means 'lock', and in yoga, it refers to a posture in which certain parts of the body are controlled or contracted in some way.

These *bandhas* must be performed whenever there is forceful holding of breath during *pranayama* practices.

When performed together, these *bandhas* unite the upward moving life-force energy [*prana*] and the downward moving life-force energy [*apana*] and direct this powerful *pranic* current into the *sushumna nadi*, to awaken the *kundalini shakti*.

The three *bandhas* which are described here, *mulabandha*, *uddiyana bandha*, and *jalandhara bandha*, can be done individually, or together, depending on the instructions of the yogic master. They are very powerful techniques for awakening the latent spiritual dynamo in each being, and should be carefully and respectfully treated.

Mulabandha [root lock]

The Sanskrit word *mula* means 'root' and refers to the region between the anus and the genitals (the perineum).

Mulabandha can also be practiced without breath retention, by itself, or as a part of certain advanced meditations, with direct oral instructions. What is given below, is the normal use of this lock, with breath retention.

Technique:

1. Sit in a comfortable posture, preferably *siddhasana* or *sukhasana*, although the former is preferred, because of the effect of the heel being pressed against the perineum, which rouses the *kundalini*.
2. Inhale slowly and deeply.
   At the same time, contract the internal and external (anal sphincter) muscles, concentrating on a point just above this sphincter muscle (perineum) and contracting it.
3. The breath is retained for a period of time, together with the contraction of the sphincter muscles.
4. Release the contraction of the internal and external sphincter muscles, and then slowly exhale.

Mulabandha can also be held with external breath retention, that is after exhalation. Whether internal or external, the forceful holding of breath, or *kumbhaka* should be held for only as long as is comfortable. Do not strain.

Benefits:
This practice strengthens the reproductive glands, and the sphincter muscles of the anus, as well as increases vitality, while at the same time helping to maintain sexual self-control.

Effects:
Normally, the senses open outwards, but with the practice of this *bandha*, they are made to flow up and inwards to meet the source – the Divine *Hamsa* Consciousness. [*Hamsa* means swan, and is the ancient *yogic* symbol for the Soul]

Uddiyana Bandha (Abdominal lock)

Uddiyana comes from the Sanskrit root 'ud' and 'di', which means 'flying up'. The *pranic* energy flies up through the *sushumna nadi* from the navel center to the higher energy centers.

It can be practiced either standing or sitting. The following description is for the standing position, which is usually easier for getting started, although for most *pranayama*, this *bandha* would be performed in the sitting position.

Technique:
1. Stand with your feet about 2 feet apart. With your knees slightly bent, grip the middle of your thighs with your hands and lean your trunk forward from the waist.
2. Inhale deeply, then exhale completely.
3. Contract and pull your whole abdominal region back towards your spine, lifting it upwards. Raise your lumbar and dorsal spine forward and upwards.
4. Retain your breath out holding the *bandha* for as long as is comfortable. Never strain or go beyond your endurance.
5. Release the *bandha* by relaxing the abdominal muscles, and return to relaxed breathing for a few breaths, then repeat the whole process again. In the beginning practice three to five abdominal lifts, gradually increasing to ten in each held breath.

Practice on an empty stomach. Early morning on rising is the best time. Do not practice if you have high blood pressure, hernia of the diaphragm, ulcers or heart ailments. Women should not practice during pregnancy or menstruation.

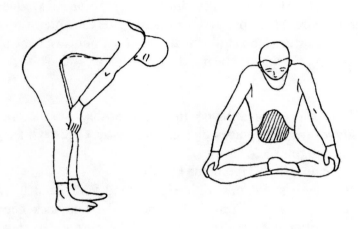

Figure 37. *Uddiyana Bandha*

Benefits:
It increases the gastric fire, and decreases indigestion and abdominal diseases.

Effects:
Exercises the diaphragm, messages and tones the muscles of the heart. It tones the abdominal organs and eliminates toxins in the digestive tract.

Jalandhara Bandha [Chin Lock]

Jala means 'net' or 'network'. In the neck there is a network of nerves and arteries which go up to the brain. *Dhara* means 'pulling upwards'.

When the chin lock is applied, pressure is placed on the carotid sinus nerve, the internal and external carotid arteries, which lie on both sides of the neck and carry blood to the brain, are also squeezed under pressure. These pressures influence the blood pressure, slow down the heartbeat and slow down the nerve impulses to the brain. This brings calmness to the mind.

Technique:
1. Sit in a comfortable posture, preferably *padmasana* or *siddhasana*, and place your palms on your knees. Close your eyes and relax.
2. Inhale deeply and retain the breath.
3. Raise your shoulders slightly and bend your head forward, pressing your chin firmly into the hollow of your neck, between your collar bones. This stretches the cervical vertebrate, stimulating the nerve centers.
4. Hold this position for as long as comfortable without strain, then slowly release the chin lock by raising the head and exhale.
5. Practice up to ten rounds, gradually increasing to 20. Do not inhale or exhale until the chin lock has been released and the head is upright.

Jalandhara Bandha should not be practiced by persons with high blood pressure or heart ailments.

Figure 38. *Jalandhara Bandha*

Effects:
Due to the lock of the *nadis* around the neck, the *ida* and *pingala* channels are pressed and the *prana* is allowed to pass through the *sushumna*. It clears the nasal passages and regulates the flow of the *prana* to the heart, head and the endocrine glands in the neck. It also relaxes the brain and humbles the ego.

Benefit:
An additional effect is that this lock prevents the subtle nectar that flows from the crown center from falling to the navel center, where it is normally burnt up by the gastric fire. This helps to prolong the life of the *yogi*, as well as giving a youthful appearance.

Tribandha (Triple Lock)

In *tribandha*, the three *bandha*s – *mulabandha, uddiyana bandha* and *jalandhara bandha* – are practiced simultaneously during retention of the breath in *pranayama*.

1. Sit in *siddhasana* or *sukhasana* with your palms on your knees.
2. Inhale deeply.
3. Perform *mulabandha, uddiyana bandha*, then *jalandhara bandha* in that order.
4. Retain your breath, holding the three *bandha*s for as long as is comfortable. Do not strain.
5. Release the *bandhas*, reversing the order: *jalandhara bandha uddiyana*, and finally, *mulabandha*.
6. Exhale slowly.

Tribandha can also be practiced with external breath retention, that is after exhalation.

Effect:
Tribandha vitalizes the whole body with *prana*, stimulates the psychic energy flow and combines all the benefits of the three individual *bandha*s.

Pranayama Variations
with forced breath retention

In the next section are descriptions of the pranayama incorporating forced holding of breath. They are given for completeness and for those who are authorized to practice with forced breath retention.

In general, the oral tradition is that holding of breath after exhalation is less harmful, but more difficult, then holding of breath after inhalation and before exhalation.

Throughout the main parts of this book, I've plainly stated that forced breath retention should only be undertaken with the close supervision of a competent and authorized master of the science of breath. This is because of the potential for physical harm, as well as emotional and mental problems, which can occur, during incorrect practice.

1. Sukha Pranayama

These are done with both nostrils and with equal length of the inhalation and exhalation.

Variation 1: Sukha anuloma

This should be practiced under supervision, as it involves breath retention. It is a three-part equal breath ratio: inhale for six, retain for six, and exhale for six (6:6:6:0). Practice a minimum of seven rounds. During breath retention, apply all three *bandhas*.

Variation 2: *Sukha viloma*

This should be practiced under supervision, as it involved breath retention. It is also a three part equal breath ratio: inhale for six, exhale for six, and external retention for six (6:0:6:6). Practice seven rounds. During breath retention, apply all three *bandhas*.

Variation 3: *Sukha purvaka*

This is a combination of the two previous variations, and should be attempted, only after achieving proficiency in them. It is a four part equal breath ration:
Inhale for six, retain for six, exhale for six, and external retention for six (6:6:6:6).

Practice seven rounds. During breath retention, apply all three *bandhas*.

2. *Suryabheda variation with forced breath retention*

Raise your right hand and place your fingers in *nasik mudra*. Close your left nostril with your ring and little fingers. Inhale slowly, deeply, quietly, and with total awareness through your right nostril.

Close both nostrils and retain your breath. Apply the chin lock (*jalandhara bandha*), navel lock (*uddhiyana bandha*), the anal lock (*mulabandha*). Hold your breath without straining, for at least a count of 12.

Release *mulabandha* first, then *uddhiyana bandha* and finally, *jalandhara bandha*. Then, exhale slowly, deeply and quietly through your left nostril. This completes one round. Without pausing, close your left nostril and again inhale through your right nostril. Perform seven rounds.

3. *Chandrabheda variation with forced breath retention*

Raise your right hand and place your fingers in *nasik mudra*. Close your right nostril with your thumb. Inhale slowly, deeply, quietly, and with total awareness through your left nostril.

Close both nostrils and retain your breath. Apply the chin lock (*jalandhara bandha*), navel lock (*uddhiyana bandha*), and the anal lock (*mulabandha*). Hold your breath without straining, for at least a count of 12.

Release *mulabandha* first, then *uddhiyana bandha*, and finally *jalandhara bandha*. Then, exhale slowly, deeply and quietly through your right nostril. This completes one round. Without pausing, close your right nostril and again inhale through your left nostril. Perform seven rounds.

4. *Nadi Shuddhi with forced breath retention*

Variation 1: simple breath retention

This uses the same alternating breathing pattern as in the basic alternating breath, but with breath retention after the inhalation and before the exhalation.

The relative ratios of *puraka* (breath inhalation), *kumbaka* (retention) and *rechaka* (exhalation) are: 1:2:2:0 This means that the breath retention is twice that of the inhalation, and the period of exhalation is the same as that of the retention.

Begin with a minimum inhalation count of six and therefore a retention and exhalation of twelve, for the first week. Do not increase the count until you can practice this with comfort and ease, and take guidance from a qualified teacher. Then increase the ratio to 8:16:16.

When the breath is retained, it is important to apply the *tribandha*, or triple locks.

Start by practicing three rounds of inhaling and exhaling through the left nostril. Then perform three rounds of inhaling and exhaling through the right nostril.

Continue with three rounds of the simple alternating breathing without breath retention.

Next, inhaling through the right nostril, holding the breath for six seconds, and exhaling through the right nostril. Perform 3 rounds.

Inhaling through the right nostril, holding the breath for six seconds, and exhaling through the left nostril. Perform 3 rounds.

Inhale through the left nostril. Hold the breath inside. Exhale through the right nostril. Breathe in through the right nostril. Retain the breath inside. Exhale through the left nostril. Practice for twelve rounds, using the ratio of 1:2:2:0.

Variation 2: *Advanced alternate breathing*

> *Purakam is to inhale by left nostril*
> *for sixteen counts*
> *Kumbhakam is to retain that breath*
> *for sixty-four counts*
> *Rechakam is to exhale thereafter*
> *for thirty-two counts*
> *Thus alternate from left to right and right to left*
> *With kumbhakum in between.*
> Tirumandirum 568

This should only be attempted by those who have advanced sufficiently to be able to hold the breath comfortably with the use of *bandhas* for thirty seconds. As you progress with *pranayama* practice over several years, you will be able to the advance to the ratio of 1: 4: 2, and work up to a count of 8:32:16. Start with six rounds, adding one round each week, until you can perform twelve rounds comfortably.

After at least six months of comfortably practicing 8:32:16, then progress by adding two counts each week, to the inhalation, until you can perform twelve round of 16:64:32.

Variation 3: Complete alternate breathing

A brief description is given here for reference only. This technique should only be performed under competent personal guidance of a teacher who can provide the required oral transmission that is missing from the description.

Sit in the *siddhasana* or *padmasana*. Use the *bandhas* during breath retention.

Be aware of your heart center, and inhale through the left nostril and mentally repeat *yam*, the *bija* or seed *mantra* of the element of Air, for a count of 16 seconds.

Hold your breath until you have mentally repeated the *mantra yam* 64 times.

Exhale through the right nostril, mentally repeating *yam* 32 times.

Now move your awareness to the navel center. Inhale through your right nostril, mentally repeating *ram*, the *bija mantra* of Fire 16 times with the breath.

Hold your breath until you have mentally repeated the *mantra ram* 64 times.

Exhale through your left nostril until you have mentally repeated *ram* 32 times.

Move your awareness to the third-eye center, the point between the eyebrows.

Inhale through your left nostril, mentally repeating *OM*, the *bija mantra* of Consciousness, 16 times, with the breath.

Hold your breath until you have mentally repeated *OM* 64 times.

Exhale through your right nostril, mentally repeating *OM* 32 times.

Move your awareness to the root center. Inhale through the right nostril, mentally repeating *lam*, the *bija mantra* of Earth, 16 seconds. Hold your breath, repeating the *mantra lam* for 64 seconds. Exhale through the left nostril, mentally repeating *lam* 32 times.

Practice a minimum of 3 rounds, moving slowly to 7 rounds, then to 12 rounds.

5. *Bhastrika* with both nostrils

Sit in comfortably in *siddhasana* or *padmasana* with the spine straight. Relax and close your eyes, keeping a smile on your face.

Inhale and exhale through both nostrils vigorously and rapidly, so that the expulsions of breath follow one another in rapid succession. This will bring into rapid action both the diaphragm and the entire respiratory apparatus. One rapid inhalation and exhalation completes one *bhastrika* breath.

Practice twelve breaths, breathing out deeply on the twelve expulsion. Then take a long, slow, deep inhalation through both nostrils.

Then, hold the breath for 16 seconds or as long as is comfortable, applying *mulabandha* (anal lock), *uddhiyana bandha* (navel lock), and *jalandhara bandha* (chin lock), with your awareness and concentration at the *muladhara chakra*.

Release the chin lock, navel lock, and finally, the anal lock, and exhale slowly.

This completes one round of *bhastrika*. Practice a minimum of 7 rounds. Take a short rest between each round by taking a few normal breaths. As you progress you can gradually increase the number of breaths from twelve to 16, 20, 24 and so on up to 108 in each round. The breath retention or *kumbhaka* can also be increased gradually, but with care and proper guidance from a qualified and experienced teacher of *pranayama*.

People with high blood pressure or heart problems should not practice *bhastrika*.

Variation: Bhastrika with Alternate Nostril

Sit comfortably with a straight spine, and inhale deeply through both nostrils.

Apply *nasik mudra* and close your right nostril with your thumb. Exhale slowly and deeply through your left nostril. Then take a short inhalation through the left nostril and begin the *bhastrika* breathing in the left nostril for twelve breaths.

On the twelve expulsion, hold the breath out, and apply the three *bandhas*: *mulabandha*, *uddiyana bandha*, and *jalandhara bandha*. Hold the locks for as long as comfortable, without strain. Then release *mulabandha* first, followed by *uddiyana*, and finally, by *jalandhara*.

Inhale slowly and deeply through the left nostril and hold the breath in for as long as you can comfortably, applying the chin lock, navel lock, and anal lock. Release the locks and exhale through the left nostril.

Return to normal breathing. Take a short rest before performing the same actions with the right nostril. This completes one round. You should start with 3 rounds, increasing gradually to 12 rounds.

6. Ujjayi with breath retention

After inhaling with both nostrils in *ujjayi*, completely close the glottis and perform *tribandha,* the three locks.

Hold your breath (*kumbhaka*) for a count of 12 seconds, then release the locks, first *mulabandha*, then *uddhiyana*, and finally, *jalandhara bandha*.

Apply *nasik mudra* and close the right nostril with your thumb, exhaling slowly through the left nostril, with *ujjayi*. If you maintain a constant force of breathing, you will be able to exhale for a period double the inhalation, that is for 24 seconds.

This is one round. Perform seven rounds.

7. Sitali Pranayama

The intelligent practitioner will suck the air through
the (beak of the) tongue, perform kumbhaka as before,
and exhale through the two nostrils.
This kumbhaka is called sitali
and cures enlarged stomach or spleen,
and other conditions ill-health,
such as fever, hunger and thirst.
Hatha Yoga Pradipika 2:57,58

Stick your tongue out just past the lips and curl or fold it lengthwise to form a tube, or the beak. Inhale slowly and deeply through this tube, with a hissing sound, until your lungs are filled completely. Withdraw your tongue, retain the breath and perform *jalandhara bandha*. Hold your breath for as long as in comfortable. Release the chin lock and slowly exhale through both nostrils.

This technique can be practiced daily beginning with twelve rounds and gradually increasing to 36 rounds. It is best practiced after asana and other strenuous *pranayama* practice, because it is cooling.

8. Bhramari Pranayama with kumbakha

Inhale normally with the air producing a humming sound
like that of a male bee, and exhale much slower
than the inhalation, making the humming sound
of a female bee. Yogis perform this pranayama for long
durations to get an ecstatic state of mind.
Hatha Yoga Pradipika 2:68

Sit in one of the recommended *padmasana*, or *vajrasana*, your eyes and relax.

Inhale deeply through both nostrils while making a high pitched humming sound. Retain the breath and perform *jalandhara bandha.*

Close off your ears with your index fingers. Hold it for twelve seconds, and listen for any internal sounds and focus on the third-eye to see the internal light.

Release neck lock and lower your arms. Exhale through your nostrils with your mouth closed, making a lower-pitched sound, like the humming of a female bee, and feel this vibration in your brain.

Keep the breath out for six seconds, with the ears closed, and listen internally.

Begin with sixteen rounds and gradually increase to forty-eight.

9. Murcha Pranayama with jalandhara bandha

Sit in *siddhasana* or *padmasana* with your hands on your knees, so that you are seated firmly and steady.

Inhale slowly and deeply, taking a complete *yogic* breath, then apply the chin lock or *jalandhara bandha.* Hold the breath for as long as is comfortable, and keep your arms straight, pressing your knees with your hands.

Release the chin lock, and exhale slowly as you relax your arms.

Relax and experience the calmness and tranquility.

With the eyes open, gaze upward at the spiritual eye, the point between the eyebrows. With the eyes held steadily, hold for as long as possible. Internalize your one-pointed awareness at the spiritual eye. Allow the mind and breath to become absorbed in contemplation.

After a few minutes, take a complete *yogic* breath, and then bend your head backwards keeping your eyes open, and maintaining the concentrating at the point between the eyebrows.
Apply mulabandha, and retain the breath for as long as is comfortable, keeping your arms straight, pressing your knees with your hands.

Exhale slowly as you relax your arms and close your eyes, bringing your head back to the upright position.

Relax and experience the calmness and tranquility.

This is one round. Perform two more rounds, and then relax.

Bibliography

Feuerstein, Georg: The Yoga Tradition. Hohm Press. 1998

Feuerstein, Georg: The Yoga Sutras of Patanjali. Inner Traditions. 1989

Iyengar, BKS: Light on Pranayama. Unwin Paperbacks. 1983

Johari, Harish: Breath, Mind, and Consciousness. Destiny Books. 1989

Lysebeth, Andre Van: Pranayama. Unwin Paperbacks. 1979

Muktibodhananda, Swami: Swara Yoga. Bihar School of Yoga. 1999

Rama, Swami: Science of Breath. Himalayan Institute Press. 1998.

Ramacharaka, Yogi: The Science of Breath. Yogi Publications. 1905

Rosen, Richard: The Yoga of Breath. Shambhala. 2002

Satyananda Saraswati, Swami: Asana, Pranayama, Mudra, Bandha. Bihar School of Yoga. 1999

Sivapriyananda, Swami: Secret Power of Tantrik Breathing. Abhinav Publications. 1996

Thirumoolar, Siddhar: Thirumandiram. [Volumes 1-3]. Kriya Yoga Publications. 1993

Vasu, Rai Bahadur Srisa [Translation]: The Gheranda Samhita. Munishiram Manoharlal Publishers. 1996

Vishnu-Devananda, Swami [Commentary]: Hatha Yoga Pradipika. Motilal Banarsidass. 1999

Glossary

A

Agni. The cosmic Fire element

Ahamkara. The 'I-maker' - the individuation principle, or ego, which must be transcended for Self-realization

Ahimsa. Non-harming – an important moral discipline (*yama*)

Ajna Chakra. Third-eye; sixth energy center, in the center of the head

Akasha. Ether/space - the first of the five material elements of which the physical universe is composed

Anahata Chakra. Heart center; the fifth energy center

Ananda. Bliss - the state of utter joy, which is an essential quality of the ultimate Reality

Apana. Aspect of life-force energy in the body, functioning in excretion

Apas. The cosmic Water element

Asana. Seat - a physical posture; originally this meant only a meditation posture, but has subsequently been greatly developed in Hatha Yoga

Ashtanga. The eight-limbed comprehensive yogic system

Atman. Self - the true Self, or Spirit, which is eternal and super-conscious

Avadhuta. A Nath or Lord of Yoga who has reached the highest level cosmic consciousness

Avatar. A divine incarnation, such as Rama, Krishna from Vishnu, and Babaji from Shiva

Avidya. Ignorance - the root cause of suffering (*duhkha*)

B

Babaji. Immortal being responsible for the spiritual evolution of mankind. He works in the background, without interfering with the free-will of humanity. See also *Gorakshanath*. *Babaji* is the

Ancient of Days. He was first brought to the notice of the West in *Yogananda's* classic, 'Autobiography of a Yogi'

Bandha. A physical lock in yogic postures

Bhakta. Devotee - a disciple practicing *Bhakti-Yoga*

Bhakti. Devotion - the love of the devotee toward the Divine or the *guru*

Bija. A seed or source

Brahma. The Divine principle of Creation; Creator of the universe

Brahmacharya. The discipline of chastity, which produces *ojas*

Buddha. The 'awakened one' - designation of the person who has attained enlightenment; title of *Gautama*, the historic founder of Buddhism, who lived in the sixth century B.C.E.

Buddhi. Intellect; understanding, reason

C

Chakra. Wheel - one of the psycho-energetic centers of the subtle body

Cit. Consciousness; the super-conscious ultimate Reality

Chitta. Mind-stuff; mental substratum

D

Deva. The shining one - a male deity or a high angelic being

Devi. She who shines - a female deity or a high angelic being

Dharma. Law – right conduct

Dhyana. Meditation

Dosha. A fault; the categories of physical constitution in the medical system of *Ayurveda*

G

Goraksha. Lord of the senses ['protector of cows'] - the Immortal founder of *Hatha-Yoga*; disciple of *Matsyendranath*. See also *Gorakshanath* and *Babaji*

Gorakshanath. The formal designation for *Goraksha*, as the founder of the *Nath Sampradaya*, the ancient upholders of *Yoga Guru*. A spiritual teacher; *acarya*; literally, "he who is heavy, weighty"

H

Hamsa. Swan – the Soul; particularly for that which is being propelled by the breath

Hatha-Yoga. A major branch of Yoga, developed by *Gorakshanath*; Ha-tha is the union of the sun and moon; with emphasis on the energetic and physical tools of transformation, such as postures, cleansing techniques, and breath control

I

Ida-nadi. The energy or *prâna* current on the left side of the central channel (*sushumna-nadi*) associated with the parasympathetic nervous system and having a cooling or calming effect on the mind when activated

Ishvara-pranidhana. Dedication to the Lord – surrender to the will of the Divine; one of the *Niyamas*, or *Ashtanga*

J

Japa. The recitation of *mantras*

Jivatman. The 'individual self' as opposed to the ultimate Self (*parama-âtman*)

Jîvan-mukta. A Siddha who, while still embodied, has attained liberation (*moksha*)

Jnâna. Knowledge/wisdom

K

Kaivalya. The state of absolute freedom from conditioned existence

Kama. Desire - the appetite for sensual pleasure blocking the path to true bliss (*ananda*)

Kapha. One of the doshas; predominance of Water element in the physical body constitution

Karma. Activity of any kind; the law of karma is the law of causation

Kevala kumbakha. Spontaneous cessation of breath

Khecari-mudra. The Hatha Yoga practice of curling the tongue back against the upper palate in order to seal the life energy (*prana*)

Kosha. Any one of five "envelopes" surrounding the true Self (*atman*) and thus blocking its light – the physical body is called *annamayakosha* ['envelope made of food']

Krishna. An incarnation of God Vishnu, the God-man whose teachings can be found in the *Bhagavad-Gita*

Kriya Yoga. An evolutionary practice for Self Realization, founded by Babaji

Kumbhaka. Breath retention; a part of *Pranayama*

Kundalini-shakti. The spiritual energy, which exists in potential form at the lowest psycho-energetic center of the body [*muladhara chakra*) and which must be awakened and guided to the center at the crown (*sahasrara chakra*) for Self Realization

M

Mahamudra. Great Seal. A practice of importance in Kriya Yoga

Manas. Mind - the lower mind, which is bound to the senses

Manipura chakra. The navel or third energy center

Mantra. A sacred sound or phrase, such as *om*, with a transforming effect on the mind of the individual reciting it; to be ultimately effective, a *mantra* needs to be given in an initiatory context (*dīkshā*)

Matsyendranath. 'Lord of Fish' - Guru of Gorakshanath; a great Yogi, remembered by the Buddhists as Avalokiteshwara, the Boddhisatva of Compassion

Maya. Illusion by which the world is seen as separate from the ultimate Reality

Moksha. Release / Liberation - the condition of freedom from ignorance (*avidya*) and the binding effect of *karma*

N

Nadi. Energy Channel – there are 72,000 subtle channels through which the life force (*prana*) circulates
Nadi Shodana. Purification of the energy channels
Nadi Shuddhi. Purification of the energy channels
Nath. Lord – the Masters of Yoga
Nath Sampradaya. The tradition flowing through the mists of time, of the Lords of Yoga
Nauli. Abdominal churning exercise
Niyama. Self-restraint - the second limb of *Ashtanga*, which consists of purity (*shauca*), contentment (*samtosha*), austerity (*tapas*), study (*svadhyaya*), and dedication to the Lord (*ishvara-pranidhana*)

O

Ojas. Vitality - the subtle spiritual energy produced from sexual energy through practice
Om — the original *mantra* symbolizing the ultimate Reality

P

Paramatman. Supreme self - the truel Self, which is one, as opposed to the plurality of individuated self (*jiva-atman*) existing in the form of living beings
Paramahamsa. Supreme swan – the state of a being, between liberation and Siddhahood
Pingala-nadi. The channel of the *prâna* or life-energy on the right side of the central channel (*sushumna-nadi*) and associated

with the sympathetic nervous system and having an energizing effect on the mind when activated

Pitta. One of the *doshas*; a dominance of the Fire element in the physical constitution

Prakriti. Nature, which is unconscious or *acit*

Prana. Life-force sustaining the body; the breath as an external manifestation of the subtle life-force

Pranayama. Breath control - from *prana* and *ayama* - life/breath extension")

Pratyahara. Internalization of the senses; the fifth limb in Ashtanga

Prithvi. The cosmic Earth element

Purakha. Inhalation phase of breathing

Purusha. The true Self (*atman*) or Spirit

R

Raja-Yoga. ("Royal Yoga") — a late medieval designation of *Patanjali's* eightfold *yoga-darshana*, also known as Classical Yoga, or Ashtanga

Rajas. One of the three Gunas; principle of activity and movement

Rama — an incarnation of God *Vishnu* preceding *Krishna*; the principal hero of the *Ramayana*

Rishi. Cosmic Seer – particularly apt for the Seven *Rishis*, who have ascended to the stars to help cosmic evolution

S

Sadhana. Spiritual discipline or practice leading to perfection

Sahaja. The *sahaja* state is the natural condition, that is, enlightenment or realization

Sahasrara Chakra. The crown or seventh energy center

Samadhi. The state of Yoga; the ecstatic unitive state; there are many types of *samadhi* - *samprajnâta* (with object), *asamprajnâta* (objectless) and *sahaja*(natural state of enlightenment)

Samsara. The finite world of change, as opposed to the ultimate Reality

Samskara. The subconscious impression left behind by each will-full act, which leads to habitual reactions

Sat. Being/truth - the ultimate Reality

Sat-Guru. The Guru of Truth – capable of giving the disciple the experience of super-consciousness

Satsang. Company of Truth – being in the company of a Master of Yoga

Sattva. One of the three *gunas*; the principle of light

Shakti. Energy - the dynamic aspect of the Divine; depicted as feminine

Shaktipat. Descent of energy – the transmission of spiritual energy from a Sat-Guru, to speed up the process of Self Realization in the disciple

Shambavi. A concentration technique with eyes, open and focused on the third-eye

Shishya. Student/disciple - the initiated disciple of a *guru*

Shiva. The Auspicious One – the supreme liberating aspect of the Divine; the supreme Yogi

Shuddhi. Purification

Siddha. Perfected Being

Surya. One of the names of our Sun, the highest visible manifestation of the Creative aspect of the Divine

Sushumna-nadi. The central *prâna* or life-force channel counterpart to the physical spinal cord; the *kundalini-shakti* ascends this channel during Self Realization

T

Tapas. Austerity; the fire, heat and light from *sadhana*

Tamas. One of the three *gunas*; the principle of inertia and ignorance

U

Udana. One of the aspect of the life-force energy
Uddiyana Bandha. Navel muscular lock

V

Vayu. Air; another term used for the aspects of *prana*
Vata. One of the *doshas*; a predominance of the Air element in the body
Vidya. Knowledge/wisdom
Vishnu. The preserver - the aspect of the Divine which has had in this cycle, nine incarnations, including *Rama* and *Krishna*; the tenth incarnation *(avatar) Kalki* is coming at the close of the *kali-yuga*
Vishuddha Chakra. The throat or fifth energy center
Viveka. Discernment or discriminating aspect of wisdom
Vritti. The waves of mental disturbance
Vyana. One of the aspects of the life-force energy; the *prana* which pervades the body

Y

Yajna. Sacrifice; Yoga is an inner sacrifice through meditation and self-surrender
Yoga. The state of Union with the Divine; the path of discipline and practice to achieve Self Realization
Yogi. A Self-Realized Being; commonly used also for a practitioner of Yoga, who has not yet achieved the goal

Index of Techniques

Index

About the Author

    Rudra Shivananda is dedicated to the service of humanity through the furthering of human awareness and spiritual evolution. He teaches that the only lasting way to bring happiness into one's life is by a consistent practice of awareness and transformation.

    Rudra Shivananda is committed to spreading the message of the immortal Being called *Babaji*. He teaches the message of World and Individual Peace through the practice of *Kriya Yoga*. As a student and teacher of yoga for almost 30 years, he is trained as an *Acharya* or Spiritual Preceptor in the Indian *Nath* Tradition, closely associated with the *Siddha* tradition. He is also a member of *Babaji's Kriya Yoga* Order of *Acharyas* as well as a Reiki Master with expertise in the healing and spiritual uses of gemstones and essential oils. He lives and works in the San Francisco Bay area, and has given initiations and workshops in California, Colorado, Washington, Hawaii, Ireland, India, England and Spain.

Rudra Shivananda

Other books from Alight Publications

Dew-Drops of the Soul
Author: *Yogiraj Gurunath*
A unique compilation of poetic gems from a contemporary Himalayan Master, expressing the essence of his inner experience, as a guide and inspiration for all spiritual seekers.
[106 pages. US$15.0]

Chakra selfHealing by the power of *OM*
Author: *Rudra Shivananda*
A practical workbook on healing and spiritual evolution. Tap into the potential of the primary energy centers of the body, to eliminate depression and fatigue, relieve anxiety and stress, and calm the mind to achieve inner happiness. Learn the effective *yogic* system of tuning, balancing, color healing, rejuvenation, emotional detoxification, energization, and transcendence, with the *chakras,* in a simple, and step-by-step practice.
[140 pages. US$18.5]

Earth Peace through Self Peace
Author: *Yogiraj Gurunath*
A collection of spiritual talks or *satsangs*, answering the questions from sincere seekers of truth. A Master speaks to the soul through the doorway of the heart, opening the reader to the reality of the true Self, in spite of the limitations of human language. *Yogiraj* speaks from his own direct experience, in his own simple, direct way, clearing away all doubts and irrelevancies.
[164 pages. US$18.5]

Yogiraj Siddhanath's selfHealing with Solar Power
Author: *Rudra Shivananda*
Tap into the awesome, everpresent healing power of our life-giving Sun. Through the sincere and constant practice of the *Surya Sadhana* [solar practice], you will heal the physical body, acquire greater vitality, overcome all negativity, and also come to a greater understanding and realization of your true nature. Illustrated step-by-step instructions.
[164 pages, US$18.5]

Printed in the United States
108491LV00004B/169-192/A